ROTHERHAM
A Pictorial History

An early 19th-century view of Rotherham, based on a painting by William Cowen. The artist has seated himself at the confluence of the Rother and Don. The chimneys to the right of the bridge mark the site of an 18th-century pottery, converted into an iron foundry in the 19th century. [John Guest, *Historic notices of Rotherham* (1879)]

ROTHERHAM
A Pictorial History

Anthony P. Munford

Phillimore

1994

Published by
PHILLIMORE & CO. LTD.
Shopwyke Manor Barn, Chichester, Sussex

ISBN 0 85033 925 1

Printed and bound in Great Britain by
BIDDLES LTD.
Guildford, Surrey

List of Illustrations

Frontispiece: View of Rotherham from Bow Bridge

Introduction

Prehistory

In the mid-sixth century a group of Anglo-Saxon invaders, making their way into Britain via the Humber and the Don Valley, reached the junction of the Don and the Rother and decided that they had found the site for a town.

They were not, of course, the first settlers in the area. Knowledge of Rotherham in the prehistoric era is unfortunately scanty. Finds of flint implements at Canklow Woods point to Stone Age settlements on the Red Sandstone, above the easily flooded land of the valley bottom. Other local finds include a Neolithic hammer head from Templeborough and a Bronze Age axe from Brinsworth. These finds are insufficient to allow any speculation about the prehistoric population of the Rotherham area.

More evidence remains from the Iron Age, notably the earthworks on Wincobank Hill and in Scholes Coppice. In total bulk, the largest reminder of the Iron Age is undoubtedly the enigmatic earthworks known as the Roman Rig. Excavations have failed to find a purpose for the 10 miles of linear banks and ditches. An earthwork of this length would have been difficult to defend against a determined foe and it may have been more a boundary than a defensive line.

Rickneild Street, a principal Iron-Age north-south routeway, is known to have passed close to Rotherham although its exact course is a matter for debate. There was probably more than one trackway with travellers choosing the most suitable according to the conditions. The wet weather track would have followed the crest of the sandstone ridge north to the ford at the site of Rotherham Bridge. In dry weather, travellers could have used a low level route along the Rother Valley, crossing the Don further upstream.

There have been few opportunities for urban archaeology in Rotherham and nothing is therefore known about prehistoric occupation of the town site. Iron-Age Rotherham may have been sited at Canklow Woods. The earthworks at the crest of the woods were first recognised by Harold Copley in the 1940s. Recent work by the South Yorkshire Archaeology Service suggests an Iron-Age date for most of the remains. The site may have been occupied from the Bronze Age until the Roman era and the settlement probably covered a much larger area than the remaining earthworks.

Roman Rotherham

The Roman legions landed in the south in A.D. 43 and advanced northwards, reaching Lincoln in A.D. 50. For a period the Don became the effective northern boundary of Roman Britain. North of the Don lay the warlike kingdom of the Brigantes and it suited the Romans to exert control by supporting the Queen, Cartimandua, against her husband Venutius. A string of auxiliary forts was established to watch the Brigantian frontier and support Cartimandua. Around A.D. 54 the Fourth Cohort of Gauls was sent from Lincoln to build a fort on the Don near Rotherham.

Rotherham was probably chosen because a fort here would control the crossing of Rickneild Street over the river. The Gauls chose a low lying site on the south bank of the Don, close to the ford known later as Dead Man's Hole. The first fort, constructed in timber and earth, was rebuilt in stone in around A.D. 100. There is evidence that the fort was known to the Romans as Morbium. Over the years traces have been found of several metalled roads leading to Templeborough and connecting it with the forts at Derby, Brough, Castleford and Doncaster.

The need for a fort at Templeborough disappeared with the crushing of the Brigantian revolt of A.D. 158. A civilian settlement had grown up outside the walls and this would have continued after the legionaries had moved out. The fort was hastily refortified for a time during the late fourth century but, after the legions finally left Britain in A.D. 410, Templeborough and Rotherham sink into Dark-Age obscurity.

The Dark Ages

The Humber and the Don Valley provided an attractive route into England for the North German tribes who invaded England in the aftermath of the Roman retreat. In the mid-sixth century a group of Angles arrived at the confluence of the Don and the Rother, establishing a settlement that came to be called Rotherham—'the settlement on the Rother'. They ignored Templeborough, possibly because it was low lying and liable to flooding, and settled on a site a mile or so to the north east. Here the north-south route following the sandstone ridge from Whiston reached the Don at a fordable point. This, coupled with the old Roman east-west route along the Don, made it a natural site for a settlement.

The original homestead developed into a town with a church and, probably, a market. Rotherham lay on the frontier between Mercia and Northumbria and was almost certainly involved in the seventh-century warfare between the two kingdoms and the campaigns against the Danes in the ninth century. Strong local tradition insists that the Battle of Brunanburgh, when the English king Athelstan defeated the combined Norse and Scottish army in A.D. 937, took place in the Brinsworth/Catcliffe area.

Medieval Rotherham

Rotherham appears in Domesday Book (1086) as an established town with a church, priest and mill. William the Conqueror had given the town to his half-brother, the Earl of Mortain, supplanting the pre-Conquest owner Acun. The Earl in turn had given Rotherham to one of his retainers, Nigel Fossard. To the north, Kimberworth was a separate manor held by Roger de Busli.

It is likely that by the 11th century Rotherham had assumed the form that it was to retain until the 19th century. The parish church stood on a bluff above the river, surrounded by the houses in Church Street, High Street, Brookgate (later College Street), Bridgegate and Millgate. The church was the centre of an extensive parish stretching from Thorpe Hesley and Greasbrough in the north to Brinsworth, Catcliffe and Orgreave in the south.

During the 12th century, the manor of Rotherham was split between the families of de Vesci and de Tilli. Both halves of the manor and the church, with the Monday and Friday markets and the annual fair, were given to Rufford Abbey in the 13th century. The

Abbey thus came to control almost the whole life of the town. Rotherham was an important and profitable part of the abbey's estates and the monks seem to have been benevolent landlords. The Poll Tax returns of 1379 indicate a population of about six hundred for the medieval town.

Rotherham flowered in the late 15th century. The parish church was rebuilt in the latest style. At some time during the Middle Ages the ford was replaced with a bridge and in the 1480s a bridge chapel was added. In 1482-3 the town was embellished with the red-brick College of Jesus, founded by one of Rotherham's illustrious sons, Thomas Rotherham, Archbishop of York. He had already added the beautiful Chapel of Jesus to the parish church. Erected on the site of his birthplace, the College provided accommodation for a provost and three fellows 'in grammar, singing and the art of writing'. They were required to attend the parish church every Sunday and at all festivals, instruct the choristers and teach grammar, poetry and rhetoric. The foundation of Rotherham Grammar School was laid by the requirement that the College accept 'six of the poorer boys of these parts' to be maintained and instructed up until the age of eighteen.

The 16th and 17th Centuries

At the opening of the 16th century, the inhabitants of Rotherham could have had little inkling of the upheaval that was soon to come to their ordered world. Three hundred years of monastic control came to an abrupt end with Henry VIII's suppression of the monasteries in 1538. Along with the other Rufford Abbey estates, Rotherham passed to the Crown. As the King was more interested in money than land, the manor and church were soon sold and passed into the ownership of the Earl of Shrewsbury. Further church property was seized by the Crown in 1547 when an act for the suppression of chantries led to the closure of the College of Jesus and the despoiling of the Bridge Chapel.

The Grammar School was allowed to continue with the master's salary paid by the Exchequer. This payment fell into disuse but representation to Elizabeth I resulted in 1561 in a charter guaranteeing payment. The charitable work that had been carried out by the medieval gilds (also dissolved in 1547) was taken over by the Feoffees of the Common Lands of Rotherham who received their own royal charter in 1589. For the next 300 years the Feoffees were the nearest that Rotherham had to a town council as they were responsible for the Grammar School, the Chapel on the Bridge, water supply, the town archery butts and so on.

In the early 17th century the lordship of the manor passed to the Howard family as a result of the marriage of the Earl of Shrewsbury's daughter to the Duke of Norfolk. During the Civil War most townsfolk were supporters of Parliament. In January 1643 a force of about six hundred Cavaliers attacked the small Parliamentary garrison. May the same year saw the Earl of Newcastle's Royalist army advance on Rotherham from the north. The bridge was stoutly defended against the Earl until the ammunition ran out on the second day and the townspeople were forced to surrender. Rotherham suffered a Royalist garrison until August 1644 when Major General Crawford's force passed through the town on its way to attack the Royalist garrison of Sheffield Castle. At the end of the Civil War, Charles I was lodged in the town for a night in 1647 while being taken south as a prisoner of Parliament.

The religious monopoly of the Church of England began to break down later in the 17th century. Elizabeth Hooton, a Quaker, was imprisoned for preaching in Rotherham in 1652. In the 1660s, the vicar, Luke Clayton was ejected from his living and imprisoned for refusing to observe the Act of Uniformity. On his release he returned to Rotherham and helped to found a Unitarian congregation. They met initially in a room off Church Street, but in 1706 moved to a new chapel in Downs Row, financed by the philanthropist Thomas Hollis.

Georgian Rotherham

At the beginning of the 18th century, Rotherham was a prosperous, small market town, in no way overshadowed by Sheffield further up the Don. The population had grown to some two and a half thousand. By the end of the century, it had risen to six thousand. The markets attracted customers from a wide area and the town streets could boast a number of fine gentlemen's houses. Although there was coal mining and iron working in the area, the hand of industry had not yet cast a pall over the town. When the industry did arrive, it was concentrated mostly on the west side of the Don, leaving the town centre and suburbs on the east bank as the commercial and residential area.

The town was important enough to house regular meetings of the West Riding Court of Quarter Sessions. In 1779 the Chapel on the Bridge was converted into a gaol where prisoners could be lodged before appearing at the Sessions which were held in the new Town Hall in College Street.

In the early 18th century the fields around Rotherham were still largely unenclosed. Under the Rotherham Inclosure Award of 1764, 1,034 acres of open fields, moors and commons within the township of Rotherham were enclosed and parcelled out among the freeholders. A large share went to the Earl of Effingham as lord of the manor. Smaller acreages of unenclosed land at Masbrough and Kimberworth were enclosed in 1766 and 1800. The middle of the century also saw improvement in the local road system with the formation of turnpike trusts. The trusts took over and improved stretches of road, collecting tolls to defray the cost of maintenance. The earliest local trust was the road to Hartcliffe Hill near Penistone (1740) followed by the Bawtry and Tinsley road (1759), and the Rotherham - Pleasley Road and Tinsley and Doncaster roads (both 1764).

The parish church monopoly on the religious life of the town was further threatened by the rise of Methodism. The octagonal Methodist chapel on Bunting Croft was erected in 1760, some 18 years after John Wesley first visited the area. A break-away group established an Independent congregation at Masbrough where the Baptists also had a meeting. Education was in the hands of the Grammar School (boys only), charity schools run by the Feoffees and the Unitarians and a number of private academies.

The Industrial Revolution

The occurrence of shallow seams of coal and iron ore made it inevitable that industry would invade Rotherham. Thomas May's excavation found evidence that the Romans were smelting iron at Templeborough and the local mineral resources were exploited by Kirkstead Abbey in the 12th century. This exploitation became more sophisticated in the 16th and 17th centuries when there was a furnace at Jordan, a slitting mill at Masbrough and a steel mill at Thrybergh.

The industry's insatiable demand for charcoal fuel denuded the local woodlands and by the early 18th century the shortage of charcoal was having a limiting effect on the industry. Abraham Darby's discovery that iron could be smelted with coke and the arrival in Rotherham of the Don Navigation led to the regeneration of the industry. The Navigation offered relatively cheap transport for both bulky raw materials and finished products. It was the availability of canal transport that persuaded Samuel Walker and his brothers to move their embryo iron business from Grenoside to Masbrough and ignite the Industrial Revolution in Rotherham.

The head of the Don Navigation reached Rotherham in 1740. The Walkers moved their business to Masbrough in 1746 and were soon successful. Further land was leased from the Earl of Effingham at the Holmes where blast furnaces, foundries, slitting mills and tin plate works were established. The Walkers became expert at the difficult art of casting and boring cannon, supplying large quantities to the government during the Napoleonic Wars. They were also noted for casting the component parts of the new-fangled iron bridges. Beginning by casting a trial model of a new design by the radical Tom Paine, they progressed to manufacturing major bridges at Sunderland and Southwark.

The 19th Century

At the opening of the 19th century, the government of Rotherham was still shared between the manor court, the Feoffees and the parish officers (overseers of the poor, surveyor of the highways and parish constables). The early years of the 19th century saw responsibility for the market pass to the Proprietors of Rotherham Market, a body established by the Rotherham Markets Act of 1801. The first act of the Proprietors was to replace the old huddle of butchers' stalls with the Shambles, a permanent stone building. In the 1820s a Corn Exchange was erected in the Market Place. The same act also introduced street lighting to the town, establishing Commissioners for Lighting and Paving the Town of Rotherham.

The Poor Law Amendment Act of 1834 grouped parishes into Poor Law Unions, controlled by an elected Board Of Guardians. Rotherham became the centre of a Union that stretched northwards as far as Wath on Dearne. The Guardians erected a new workhouse on Pennyless Walk Close between Moorgate and Westgate. During the century the Workhouse was developed into a complex incorporating casual wards for vagrants, an infirmary and children's homes.

The main water supply in the town centre came from springs in Wellgate. The Rotherham Water Company, established in 1827, installed a steam engine on Quarry Hill which provided a limited and intermittent supply to parts of the town. The Rotherham Gas Light and Coke Company erected its works on the river bank to the north of the Bridge in 1833 and gas lamps soon began to oust candles and oil lamps.

The 1801 Census shows that Rotherham, Masbrough and Kimberworth had a population of almost 6,500. Fuelled largely by industrial expansion, this figure was to grow steadily throughout the century, reaching 10,500 in 1841, 19,000 in 1861 and 54,000 in 1901. To house this growing population, streets of terraced houses were erected, mostly on the Masbrough side of the Don. Within the town centre, courts of ill-lit, badly ventilated houses were squeezed onto the gardens and yards behind the shops and houses fronting the streets. As there was no proper local government in the town, sanitary arrangements lagged far behind the house building, a state of affairs that contributed to the outbreak of cholera in 1832.

Medical provision in the town was limited. There were doctors for those who could afford them and advice and medicines were available from the Dispensary, founded in 1806. There were no beds at the Dispensary and anyone in need of hospitalisation had to be taken to Sheffield. The Workhouse Infirmary was a final resort for the poor but it was not until 1872 that sufficient subscriptions were raised to open the new Rotherham Hospital in Doncaster Gate.

By 1850 Rotherham was a noisome town. William Lee, conducting a government enquiry into the sanitary state of the town in 1851, heard stomach-churning evidence about cellars flooded with sewage, endemic fever and diarrhoea. It was obvious from Lee's report that more formal local government was needed to solve the town's problems. The result was the formation of the Rotherham and Kimberworth Local Board of Health in 1852. Establishing offices in Howard Street, the Local Board set to work to improve the town. One of their first actions was to take over the Water Company. A new pumping station was erected in Frederick Street and new sources of supply were obtained from Ulley and Dalton. The Gas Company was taken over in 1870 and the markets in 1869.

Until mid-century, expansion northwards from the town centre was hampered because much of the land was owned by the Earl of Effingham. The terms of a family settlement prevented the Earl from granting leases of more than 21 years, too short to attract builders. A private act of Parliament in 1850 gave him the power to grant long leases and he began to develop the land for building, laying out Effingham, Frederick and Howard Streets. At the same period, further expansion took place with the sale of building plots on the Eastwood Estate.

The intellectual life of the town was taken care of by the Literary and Scientific Society, the Ivanhoe Club (a middle-class debating society), a subscription library and the Mechanics' Institute. Opened in 1853, the Institute provided a range of educational classes, but the initial enthusiasm soon waned and the building was sold to the Corporation in 1892 for inclusion in the Town Hall. Parliamentary elections in 19th-century Rotherham were lively affairs. In 1868 and 1871 the Conservative headquarters in the *Crown Inn* on the High Street were attacked by a Liberal mob and troops had to be called to restore order.

New schools were established to deal with the growing population. A British School (Nonconformist) was constructed in Rawmarsh Road in 1833 and the Methodists opened a day school in 1860. The established church opened a number of National Schools; at Kimberworth (1830), the town centre (1848), Masbrough (1864) and Eastwood (1870). An elected School Board was established in 1875 under the terms of the 1870 Education Act. The Board began to build schools, starting with Thornhill and Westgate in 1879. Sub-standard schools, such as the Feoffees' and Hollis's, were taken over and closed as soon as modern schools were opened.

A petition from the inhabitants to Queen Victoria resulted in a royal charter of 29 August 1871, awarding Rotherham borough status. At the first meeting of the new Borough Council in November, John Michael Habershon, formerly Chairman of the Local Board, was chosen as Rotherham's first Mayor. The Corporation continued the work begun by the Local Board. A covered market hall was erected on the Market Place in 1879. When this burned down in 1888, it was replaced with a new market hall that was to serve the town until 1971. Powers to run a public library service were adopted in 1880 and a purpose-built library, combined with swimming baths, was opened on Main Street in 1887. The recreational needs of the population were supplied by the opening of Boston Park in 1876 and Clifton Park in 1891. A borough police force was established in 1882 consisting of a Chief Constable with 30 officers and men. The Chief Constable was given responsibility for the new, permanent fire brigade in 1901.

By the middle of the century, it had become obvious that the parish church could no longer minister effectively to a parish the size of Rotherham. Several daughter churches were erected to serve the outer areas, such as Thorpe Hesley, Kimberworth, Masbrough and Eastwood. These soon became independent parishes. New Nonconformist places of worship were erected to serve the growing congregations of the Methodists, Primitive Methodists, United Methodists, Congregationalists, Baptists and Plymouth Brethren.

The Assembly Rooms had been turned into a temporary Catholic church to minister to the Irish navvies building the railways in the area c.1840. The first permanent Catholic church, St Bede's at Masbrough, was opened in 1843. The parish church itself was restored in 1873-5 by the architect Gilbert Scott.

Early in the century, public entertainment was confined to visiting companies of actors who performed in the Assembly Rooms. A number of local public houses had concert rooms. The first proper theatre was the Alexandra Music Hall (later Theatre Royal) established in the former Zion Chapel in Howard Street in 1860. A purpose-built Theatre Royal, opened in Effingham Street in 1873 to bring high-class drama to Rotherham, was not a success and closed in 1892. A third theatre of the same name was built on Howard Street in 1894. There were numerous public houses in the town but there was also a strong temperance movement. Non-alcoholic refreshment was available at the Workmen's Coffee and Cocoa House in Wellgate and at St George's Hall in Effingham Street.

We have seen how the arrival of the Don Navigation in Rotherham in 1740 led directly to the expansion of industry in the area. The canal remained an important means of transport for goods until the middle of the 19th century when the new railway system began to steal the trade. By 1857 the canal was carrying over 400,000 tons of coal per year but the railways in the Don Valley were carrying twice the tonnage.

The first railway in the area was the Sheffield and Rotherham Railway, opened from the Wicker to Westgate in 1838. At Masbrough the S.R.R. crossed and connected with George Stephenson's North Midland Railway which was advancing northwards from Derby towards Leeds. There were frequent fights between the rival gangs of navvies working on the two lines. The North Midland line, with its Rotherham station at Masbrough, opened in 1840 and both railways became part of the Midland Railway in 1846.

The Don Navigation was taken over by the South Yorkshire Railway in 1849 and the South Yorkshire Railway was in turn absorbed by the Manchester, Sheffield and Lincolnshire Railway. In the mid-1860s the M.S.L.R. began to build a line to Doncaster, utilising the canal bed through Rotherham to enable the line to pass under the S.R.R. The line opened to Rotherham Central station in 1868 and was extended to Doncaster in 1871.

Industrial Expansion

The Walker family enterprises prospered during the Napoleonic Wars, but in the early 1820s the family took a hard look at the prospects for trade in the post-war era and decided that they were gloomy. Their decision, to close down their Rotherham operations and concentrate on the works at Gospel Oak in the Black Country, could have had disastrous results for Rotherham. Luckily almost all the former Walker enterprises were taken over, often by former Walker employees, and continued in operation to keep Rotherham in the forefront of the iron and steel trades.

The 19th century saw Rotherham with a very diverse economy. Many of the kitchen ranges, fireplaces, stoves and railings which embellished Victorian buildings came from Rotherham foundries such as Yates, Haywood and Co., George Wright's or Micklethwaite's. The Midland Iron Company was renowned for the production of wrought iron. Water and gas supplies flowed though taps, valves and meters from Guest and Chrimes. Medicines came in bottles from Beatson Clark's glassworks. Meals were eaten off earthenware from the Holmes and Northfield potteries. Railways at home and abroad would have ground to a halt without the wheels and axles made in Rotherham by Owen and Dyson or John Baker. All this industry was fuelled by coal from local pits.

Above all Rotherham came to be known as a steel town. The former Walker blast furnaces at the Holmes were taken over by the Park Gate Iron and Steel Company whose main works were just outside the borough. But it was the works of Steel, Peech and Tozer Ltd. that came to dominate much of the life of Rotherham. Their works at Ickles and Templeborough, founded in 1875, eventually stretched for a mile along Sheffield Road. It was the installation of 14 open hearth furnaces at the Templeborough works to meet wartime demands that led to the excavation of the Roman fort in 1917. The following year Steel, Peech and Tozer joined with Samuel Fox and Company of Stocksbridge, Appleby Frodingham Steel Company of Scunthorpe and the Workington Iron and Steel Company to form the United Steel Companies Ltd. The works at Templeborough expanded steadily until, in the early 1960s, with a total workforce of 8,500, Steel, Peech and Tozer was by far the largest employer in the town.

The 20th Century

The town attained County Borough status in 1902. The Education Act of the same year transferred the powers of the School Board to the Corporation. The private Girls' High School on Alma Road was taken over by the Corporation in 1903, with new premises in Middle Lane erected in 1910. The Grammar School was put on a new footing in 1904, with the majority of governors being nominated by the Corporation. Higher elementary schools, for pupils aged 11 to 14, were opened at South Grove (1911) and Kimberworth (1914).

Electric light and power arrived in 1903 as a result of the introduction of electric trams. The new tram routes resulted in a number of road improvements, including the widening of High Street (1907) and the construction of Corporation Street (1913). As part of the High Street widening, the Shambles was demolished and replaced with Imperial Buildings.

During the 19th century public transport on local roads was confined to coach and wagon services to local villages and towns. The Corporation obtained parliamentary powers to run trams in 1900 and the first tram services ran in January 1903. Connections with the Sheffield and the Mexborough and Swinton tramway systems allowed through running. Trolleybuses were introduced in 1912, initially on a service from the Broom tram terminus to Maltby. The first motor buses were purchased in 1913. By the 1930s a number of tram routes had been converted to trolleybus operation. The last trams, on the Templeborough route, ran in 1949 and the final trolleybus trip came in 1965. In 1974 control of the bus services passed from the Corporation to the new South Yorkshire Passenger Transport Executive.

The growing desire for entertainment was served by the opening of new large theatres, the Hippodrome on Henry Street in 1908 and the Empire on High Street in 1913. Both later became cinemas. The first purpose-built cinema was the Picture Palace (later Whitehall) in the High Street, opened in 1911. This was soon followed by others; the Electric Pavilion (a converted chapel), opened later in 1911, and the Cinema House on Doncaster Gate (1914). Those living on the other side of the river were served by the Premier Picture Palace (1912) and the Tivoli (1913).

When war broke out in 1914, many local factories were turned over to war production. As men were called up, the factories began to recruit women to replace them. The pages of the *Rotherham Advertiser* soon began to carry the names and photographs of the many local men who had been killed. The local regiment, the York and Lancaster, suffered particularly heavy casualties on the Somme in 1916. When work began in 1919 to draw up a list of names to be inscribed on the war memorial in Clifton Park, the list ran to 1,304 names.

Immediately the war ended, the Corporation began to exercise its powers to build houses for rent. A site on Doncaster Road was chosen, with the first sod being cut in July 1919. The first tenant moved into his council house on the East Dene Estate in May 1920. By 1939 the Council had built over 5,000 dwellings, 25 per cent of the houses in the town. With this supply of new houses, the Council was able to start condemning and demolishing slum houses and large numbers were swept away in the 1930s. The construction of council houses was paralleled by widespread building of private houses on the outskirts of the town.

Rotherham was not exempt from the Depression of the 1920s and 1930s, and in 1930 the town was designated a depressed area. During the 1930s Herringthorpe Valley Road and Meadow Bank Road were constructed to provide employment. Many other changes took place between the wars. In 1923 the Prince of Wales (later Edward VIII) visited Rotherham to open the new Power Station. Bow Bridge was reconstructed in 1927 and Chantry Bridge was built to replace the medieval bridge in 1930. A new Court House on the Crofts necessitated the removal of the Cattle Market to Corporation Street in 1926. Bridgegate was widened in 1928 and All Saints Square became the main bus and trolleybus terminus.

Local factories turned over to war production once again in 1939 and women were once more employed to replace men who were in the forces. The local workers turned out to patrol with the Home Guard or A.R.P. after work. Women served in the W.V.S. and faced the weekly problem of devising interesting meals from the rations. Both sexes spent long hours fire watching. Although there were 142 alerts during the war, there were only two serious air raids when houses in the Holmes area were destroyed during two nights in August 1940. The town raised £5,000 to buy a Spitfire and a further £700,000 to adopt the destroyer HMS *Rotherham*. Several local firms manufactured components for the war-winning Bailey Bridge, designed by Rotherham-born Donald Bailey.

After the celebrations of VE and VJ Days, the town tried its best to return to normal despite the post-war austerity. The Corporation restarted its house building programme, developing new estates at East Herringthorpe, Broom Valley and Kimberworth Park. By 1967, over 6,000 houses had been erected since 1945.

During the 1960s the appearance of the town began to change. A local landmark disappeared when the 14 chimneys of the Templeborough Melting Shop were demolished and the open hearth furnaces were replaced with six electric arc furnaces. Steel, Peech and Tozer itself was to disappear shortly afterwards when the steel industry was nationalised. Property in the Rawmarsh Road and St Ann's area was demolished to make way for the first phase of an inner ring road, opened in 1969.

The Corporation celebrated its centenary in 1971. In the same year over 700 years of history came to an end when the Market Place was moved from its traditional site to the new Centenary Markets constructed on the site of the Hippodrome. The Borough Council itself was only to last for three more years. On 1 April 1974, Rotherham ceased to be a County Borough of 85,000 people and became the centre of the new Rotherham Metropolitan Borough with a population of 250,000.

Acknowledgements

All the illustrations in this book are taken from the collections of the Archives and Local Studies Section of Rotherham Central Library. The section's Illustrations Collection now stands at some 11,000 photographs relating to places within the Metropolitan Borough of Rotherham. Thanks are due to the many people who have generously donated originals or have allowed photographs to be copied. The Section is always happy to hear from members of the public who have single photographs or collections which they are prepared to donate or have copied.

Particular thanks are due to the following people who have allowed illustrations still in copyright to be used:

Mr. R. Cogill, no. 125; Tiny Gittins, nos. 14, 27, and 163; Mrs. J.M. Habershon, no. 43; South Yorkshire Archaeology Service and Rotherham Borough Council, Department of Planning, no. 2 (project funded by the Department of the Environment); Denis Grayson, no. 44.

N.B. The figure in square brackets at the end of each caption is the Archives and Local Studies Section reference number of that photograph.

> *This book is dedicated to Linda, Claire and Peter*
> *who have put up with being wordprocessor widow and orphans*
> *with the minimum of complaint and a constant supply of tea.*

1 Evidence of prehistoric navigation in the Don Valley was revealed in 1964 when this boat was uncovered during building work in Chapel Dike Flat at Templeborough. Carbon dating indicated a date of approximately 1500 B.C., in the early Bronze Age. The boat is now at Weston Park Museum, Sheffield. [112/B]

2 The earthworks in Canklow Woods are difficult to interpret. First recognised by Harold Copley in the 1940s, they are now thought to be the remains of an Iron-Age farming community. [*Archaeology in South Yorkshire 1991-1992*, South Yorkshire Archaeology Service (1992)]

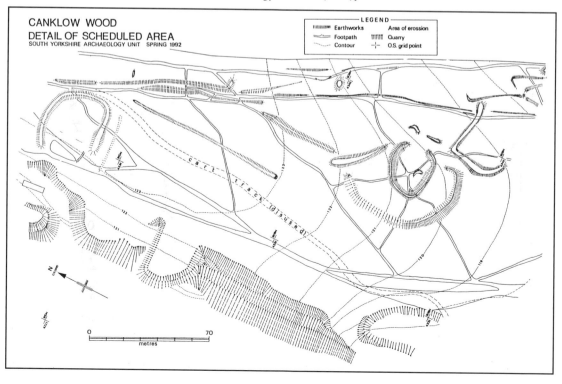

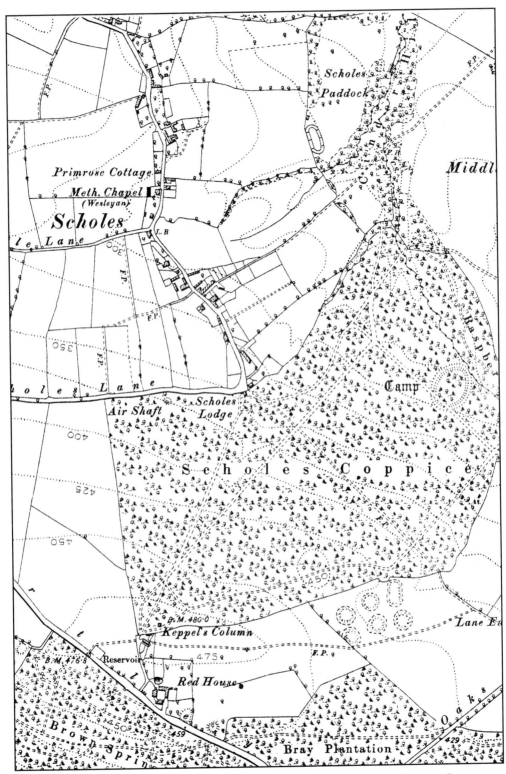

3 In places the banks of the camp in Scholes Wood still reach a height of two to five metres above the ditch and enclose an area of 0.35ha. Although known locally as 'Caesar's Camp', recent archaeological investigation has confirmed an Iron-Age date. The trees that now cover the site are the result of 18th-century landscaping on the Wentworth Woodhouse estate. [Ordnance Survey 1:10560, sheet 289NW]

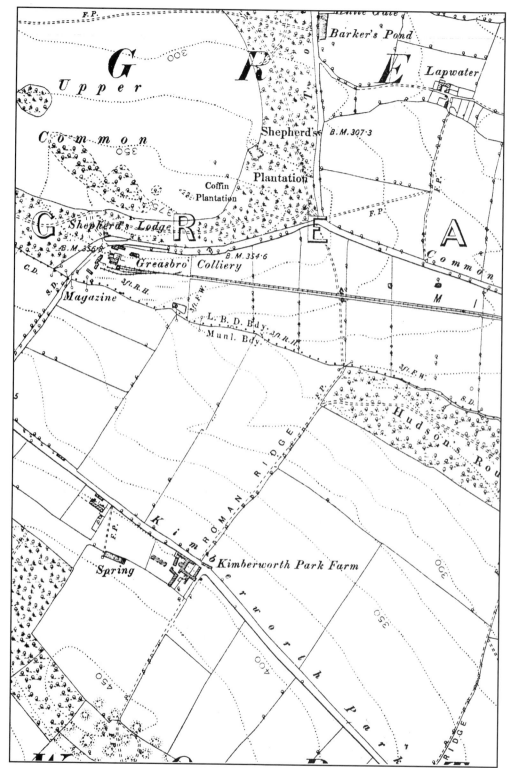

4 The double line of banks and ditches known as 'the Roman Rig' extends for some ten miles from the hill fort at Wincobank towards Kilnhurst and Mexborough. Excavations have failed to reveal the exact age and purpose of the earthworks. They probably date from the Iron Age and may have been intended more as a boundary than a defensive line. [Ordnance Survey 1:10560 sheet 289NW]

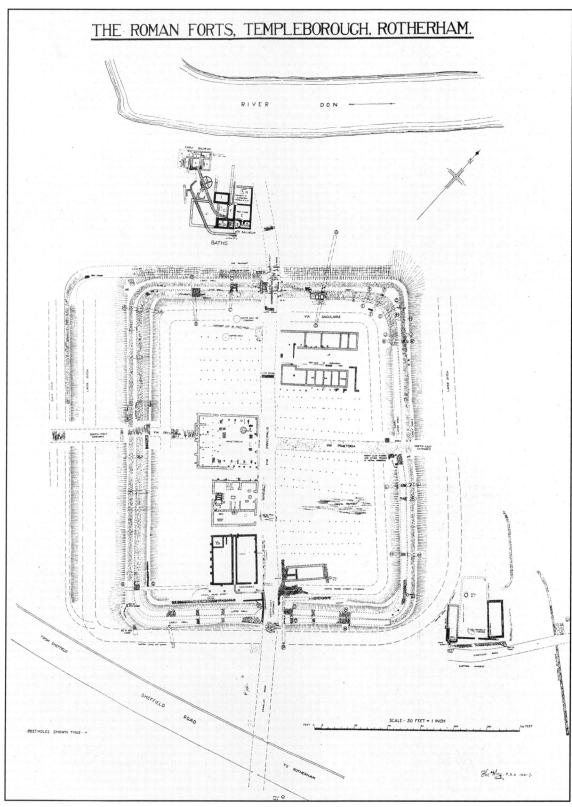

THE ROMAN FORTS, TEMPLEBOROUGH, ROTHERHAM.

5 The full plan of the three forts on the site was revealed by Thomas May's excavation of 1916-7. The original wood and earth fort had been rebuilt in stone around A.D. 100 and hastily rebuilt in the fourth century. May's excavation took place just before the site disappeared beneath Steel, Peech and Tozer's Templeborough Melting Shop in 1917. [May, T., *The Roman forts of Templeborough near Rotherham* (1922)]

6 The name 'Templeborough' was applied to the fort site as early as the 13th century and it was a handy source of building stone for centuries. The first excavations were carried out in 1877-8 by members of the Rotherham Literary and Scientific Society. Among the remains uncovered were this column and column base. [4130]

7 The 1877-8 excavations uncovered a number of tiles stamped 'G IIII G' which enabled the building of the first fort to be ascribed to the Fourth Cohort of Gauls. This force was probably about a thousand strong and was among the auxiliary forces that had accompanied the invading legions. [4134]

8 The surviving columns of the fort's granary were removed by Thomas May and subsequently re-erected at the rear of the Museum in Clifton Park. [1944]

In Rodreham hb dcun .i. maner̄ de .v. carucat̄
ad gld. ubi poss. ẽẽ. iii. car̄. Nigel hẽ ibi in dño .i. car̄.
7 viii. uilt 7 iii. bord̄ hntes .ii. car̄ 7 dimid. 7 i. molt̄
x̄ solidoȓ. pbr̄ 7 ęccla. p̃a .iii. ac̄ Silua past̄. ou ac̄.
Toũ xx. quar̄ lg. 7 v. quar̄ 7 dim̄ lat̄. T.R.E. uat. iiii. lib.
m̄ .xxx. sot̄.

9 Domesday Book (1086) provides the earliest word picture of Rotherham ('Rodreham'—the settlement on the Rother). Nigel Fossard was lord of the manor as tenant of the Earl of Mortain. There was land for three plough teams, eight villeins, a mill worth 10s., a priest and a church. The town's value was assessed at 30s.

10 It is tempting to think that the house shown on the banks of the Don, between 'Sheffeld' and 'Doncastre' on Gough's map of Britain (*c*.1325-50), marks Rotherham. The Don—Fluvius Done—is shown taking a strange course beyond Sheffield towards Chesterfield. The only roads shown are the Great North Road through Doncaster (with a branch to Wakefield) and a road along the south bank of the Don. [O.S. facsimile, pub. 1935]

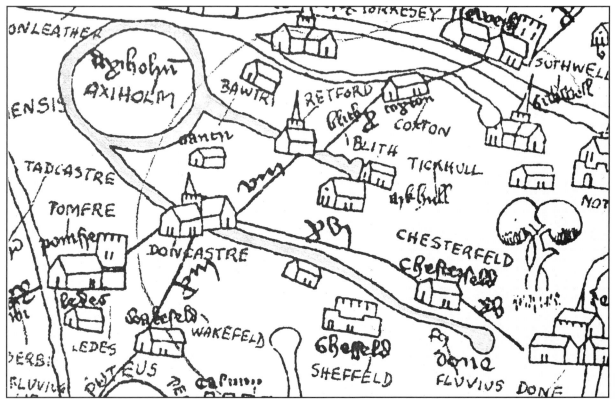

11 The most enduring reminder of medieval Rotherham is the parish church of All Saints' which dominates the town centre. A few fragments of Saxon work remain within the church but the church we see now is the result of substantial rebuilding by the monks of Rufford Abbey in the 15th century. [Guest, J., *Historic notices of Rotherham* (1879)]

12 The stalls in the chancel bear a fine set of carved finials or 'poppy heads' at their ends. These tell the stories of the Annunciation and the Adoration of the Magi. The Virgin Mary exhibits the infant Jesus to the world. [1728]

13 Rotherham's medieval vicarage, shown in this late 18th-century drawing, faced onto the churchyard. The vicarage is the building on the right. The house on the left was demolished in the 1790s for the enlargement of the churchyard. A new vicarage was constructed on Moorgate in the early 19th century. [2951]

14 The oldest secular building remaining in the town centre is the former *Three Cranes* inn, occupied by Wakefields in this 1963 view. Freeman, Hardy and Willis rebuilt their half of this 15th-century timber-framed building later in the decade. Sadly the *Three Cranes* has lain empty for over ten years. [7783]

15 The ford across the Don was replaced by a bridge at an unknown date in the Middle Ages. The present structure dates from the late 15th century. Originally there were only four arches, a mere 15 feet wide between the parapets. The bridge was widened on the upstream side in 1768 and extended westwards to accommodate a shift in the course of the river. [2628]

16 The chapel on Rotherham Bridge is one of only three that still exist in Britain. Erected in 1483 and richly endowed, it enabled travellers to say prayers before a long journey and to give thanks for a safe arrival in Rotherham. Its furnishings included a golden statue of the Virgin and Child.

17 Thomas Scot, more frequently known as Thomas Rotherham (1423-1500), was born in Rotherham. Educated in the town and later at Eton and Cambridge, he entered the Church and rose rapidly to become in turn Bishop of Rochester, Bishop of Lincoln and finally, in 1480, Archbishop of York. He was Lord Chancellor of England on three occasions. [896]

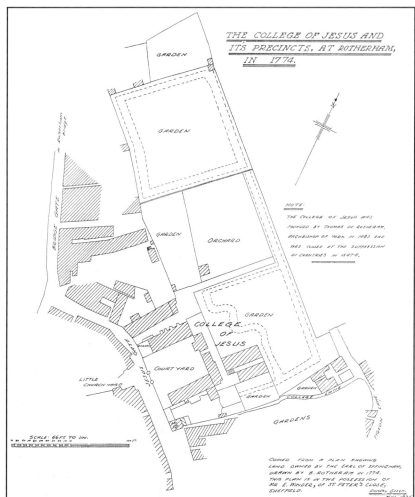

THE COLLEGE OF JESUS AND ITS PRECINCTS, AT ROTHERHAM, IN 1774.

NOTE:
THE COLLEGE OF JESUS WAS FOUNDED BY THOMAS DE ROTHERHAM, ARCHBISHOP OF YORK IN 1483 AND WAS CLOSED AT THE SUPPRESSION OF CANTRIES IN 1547-6.

GARDEN

GARDEN

GARDEN

ORCHARD

COLLEGE OF JESUS

COURTYARD

LITTLE CHURCH YARD

GARDEN

GARDEN

COLLEGE

GARDENS

SCALE; 66FT. TO 1IN.

COPIED FROM A PLAN SHOWING LAND OWNED BY THE EARL OF EFFINGHAM, DRAWN BY B. ROTHERAM IN 1774. THIS PLAN IS IN THE POSSESSION OF MR E. WINDER, OF ST. PETER'S CLOSE, SHEFFIELD.

Dorothy Greene. May, 1935.

18 The College of Jesus in Brookgate (College Street) was Archbishop Rotherham's greatest gift to his native town. Founded in 1481-2, the buildings were turned to secular uses after suppression in 1547. Fragments of medieval brickwork still survive within the walls of Woolworths and one doorway survived to be re-erected in Boston Park in 1876.

19 Kirkstead Abbey Mews dates back to the 12th century when the monks of Kirkstead Abbey (Lin) were granted land on the Kimberworth/Ecclesfield border. Here they established a grange to mine and smelt the local iron ore. The buildings are shown here during restoration in 1900. [4267]

20 The fact that in 1207 King John granted Eustace de Vesci the right to hold a fair in Rotherham suggests that there was already a market in existence. The town's medieval market place remained in use until 1971. This view shows the Market Cross, medieval Town Hall and stocks. [Guest, J., *Historic notices of Rotherham* (1879)]

21 At some time after the closure of the College of Jesus in 1547, the southern wing was converted into the *College Inn*. This building survived until 1930 and substantial portions of the original were incorporated into the new *College Inn*, built in 1930. [Guest, J., *Historic notices of Rotherham* (1879)]

22 Among the most influential families in the town during the 16th century were the Swifts. This fine brass commemorating Robert Swifte (d.1561), his first wife Anne (d.1539) and their four children is in the parish church. His eldest son, Robert Swift II, acted as seneschal to the Earl of Shrewsbury. [1565]

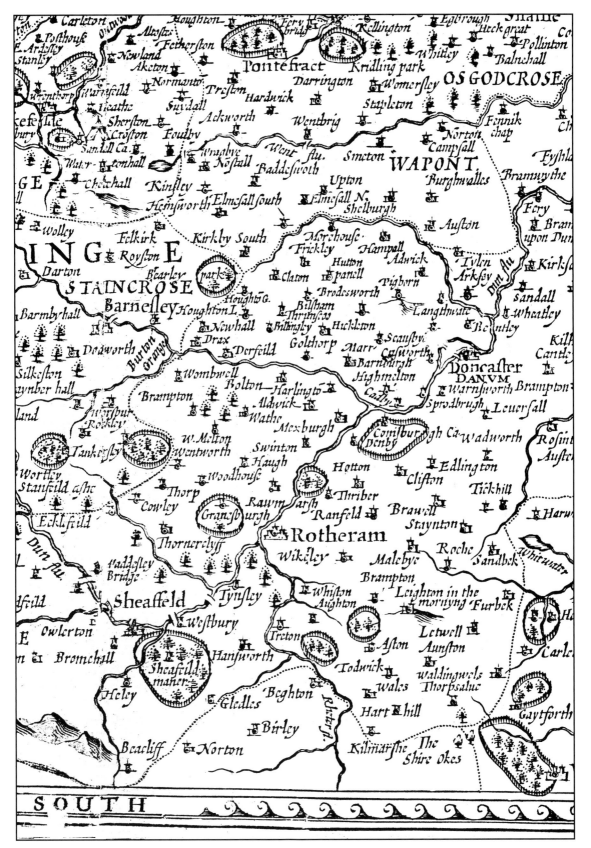

23 John Speed's 1610 map of the West Riding shows towns and rivers but not roads, as was normal at that period.

Vera Effigies Patris ROBERTI Lincolniensis   Reverendi SANDERSON Episcopi Æt 76 1681.

24 Robert Sanderson (1587-1663) was the son of Robert Sanderson of Guilthwaite Hall and is thought to have been born in Rotherham. After education at Rotherham Grammar School and Lincoln College, Oxford, he entered the Church. Sanderson was appointed a chaplain to Charles I in 1631, Regius Professor of Divinity at Oxford in 1642 and Bishop of Lincoln in 1660. [932]

25 Charles Hoole (1610-67), a protégé of Robert Sanderson, was appointed master of Rotherham Grammar School in the 1630s. He was a noted expert on the theory and practice of education, writing several text books, including *The Latine Grammar fitted for use in schools* of 1665.

Hgr.   Pag. 1.   A. F.

THE
LATINE GRAMMAR
FITTED FOR
THE USE OF SCHOOLS.
WHEREIN
The Words of *Lilie's* Grammar are (as much as might be) retained ; many errors thereof amended; many needless things left out: many neceſſaries that were wanting, ſupplyed ; and all things ordered in a Method more agreeable to Childrens capacitie.

By *Charles Hoole*, Mr. of Arts of Lincoln-Colledge in *Oxford*, ſometime School-maſter of *Rotheram* in *York-ſhire*.

And (that nothing might be wanting to the purpoſe) The Engliſh Tranſlation is ſet down on the contrarie page for the benefit of Young-learners.

The fourth Edition more exactly Corrected than the former Impreſſions.

FRANC. PATRI.
Grammar is the Foundation of all Diſciplines.

LONDON,
Printed by *R. J.* for *F. Smith* at the *Caſtle* and *Elephant* without Temple-Barre.   1665.

GRAMMATICA LATINA
IN
USUM SCHOLARUM
ADORNATA.

Grammatices Lilianæ verbis (quantum fieri licuit) retentis; multis ejus erroribus [emendatis; minus-neceſſariis amputatis; pluribus, quæ deficerent, ſuppletis; & omnibus Methodo faciliori ad tenellæ ætatis captum conformata diſpoſitis.

Opera & Studio CAROLI HOOLE A. M.
è C.L. *Oxon.* Scholarchæ olim *Rotherhamienſis* in agro *Ebor.*

Adjecta eſt inſuper (nè quid huic inſtituto deſit) in juventutis gratiam, in adverſa paginâ, Anglicana interpretatio.

Editio quarta prioribus emendatior.

FRANC. PATRI.
Grammatica eſt omnium Diſciplinarum Fundamentum.

LONDINI,
Excudebat *R. I.* pro *F. Smith*, ad *Caſtellum* & *Elephantum* extra Temple-Bar. 1665

26 Moorgate Hall was built by Charles Tooker in 1627. The house was remodelled in the 18th century but retains its 17th-century staircase. In the 18th century it was the home of the Tooker family. The Hall remained a private home until the 1980s but is now used as offices. [5743]

27 Wellgate Old Hall seems to have originated as a 14th-/ 15th-century timber building encased in local sandstone in the 17th century. It has been suggested that the Hall was the manorial base of Rufford Abbey in the town. In the 19th century the building was divided into four cottages and its archaeological history was only uncovered during conversion to offices in the early 1980s. [7795]

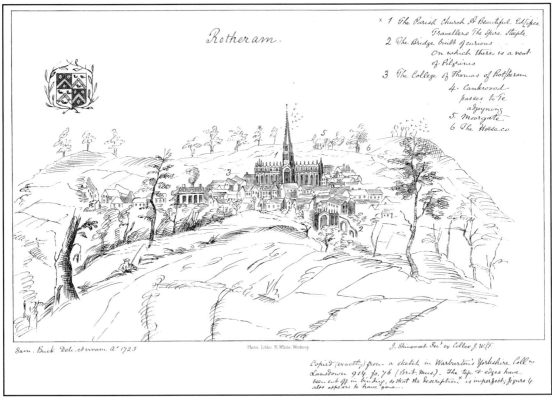

Rotheram.

Sam. Buck Deli. et vivam a° 1723.   Photo. Litho. R.White. Worksop   J. Shinewick Fec.¹ ex Collec J. W.C⁵

28 The first topographical view of Rotherham is this sketch by the artist Samuel Buck, made in 1723. It shows the town from the north, clustered around the church. The sketch was intended as the basis for an engraving that was never made.

29 Thomas Harris chose a similar viewpoint to Buck for his engraved view of the town *c.*1740. It shows Rotherham just before the expansion of industry led to growth on the Masbrough bank of the river.

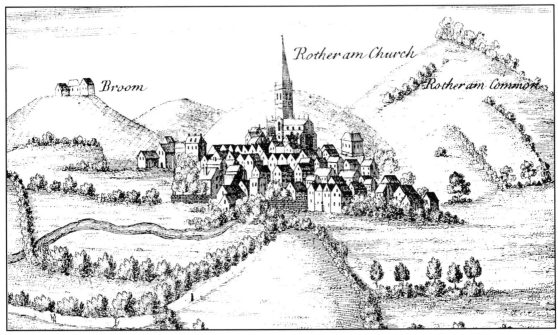

Broom

Rotheram Church

Rotheram Common

30 The Rotherham base of the Earls of Effingham and their predecessors was a relatively modest house at the Holmes. They retained this until *c*.1770 when the surrounding industrialisation forced a move to the countryside. [*Ivanhoe Review*, vol. II (1899)]

The Old Holmes Hall

31 The Earl moved from the Holmes to this new house, Thundercliffe Grange, designed by the York architect John Carr in 1771. The third storey was added later. Today the artist would be sitting in the middle of the M1. [4949]

32 Ferham House at Masbrough was designed *c.*1775-80 by the Rotherham mason/architect John Platt for Jonathan Walker II (d.1807), a member of the prominent iron founding family. The sundial in the foreground was one of a number made by Jonathan's uncle, Samuel Walker I, and is now in Clifton Park. [4806]

33 Purpose-built commercial premises were uncommon in the 18th century. The lawyer, Ralph Tunnicliffe, who numbered the Walkers among his clients, built these offices on Snail Hill in 1777. The building was used by Tunnicliffe's successors-in-practice until 1887 and is now a restaurant. [4193]

34 Samuel Buck II (1746-1806) was another prominent 18th-century lawyer. A leading barrister on the north-east circuit, he served as Recorder of Leeds. Buck's memorial in the Parish Church is by the noted sculptor John Flaxman. The family's town house still stands in Bridgegate, now occupied by Poundstretcher. [1574]

35 The first Nonconformist congregation in the town were the Presbyterians or Unitarians who met initially in a room off Church Street and later in this chapel in Down's Row, built in 1706. The site for the chapel was given by Thomas Hollis who had established a charity school in the town in 1702. [373]

36 John Wesley preached in Rotherham on a number of occasions. The local Methodist congregation met initially in William Green's house. The first chapel, octagonal in shape, was erected on Bunting Croft in 1761. It was replaced by a more conventional building in 1805. [Guest, J., *Historic notices of Rotherham,* 1879]

37 Rev. John Thorpe led a break-away from the Methodists to found an Independent congregation. Samuel Walker donated a site next to his house at the Yellands, Masbrough, and the new chapel opened in 1763. The chapel was rebuilt in 1780 and still stands but is now used as a carpet warehouse. The chapel yard contains the mausoleum of the Walker family. [4464]

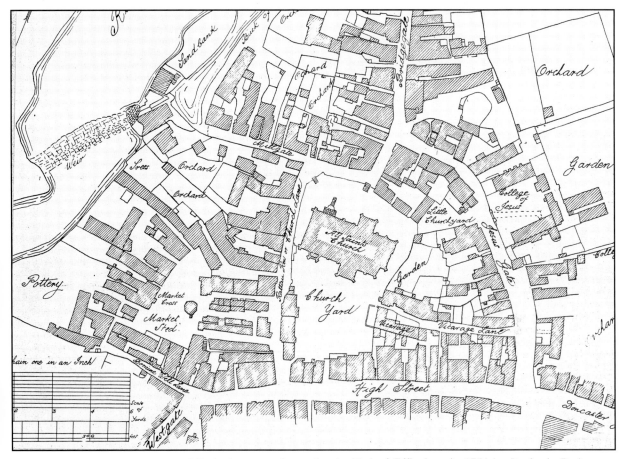

38 The first known town map of Rotherham was drawn for the Earl of Effingham in 1774 by Benjamin Rotheram, master of the Feoffees' School. The original map is now lost but fortunately a number of copies were made in the 1930s.

39 The Don Navigation, a combination of side cuts and improved river stretches, reached Rotherham in 1740 and Tinsley in 1751. The Navigation enabled bulk loads to be imported and exported via the Humber with relative ease. This plan of 1804 shows a proposed extension of the Eastwood Cut to Aldwarke.

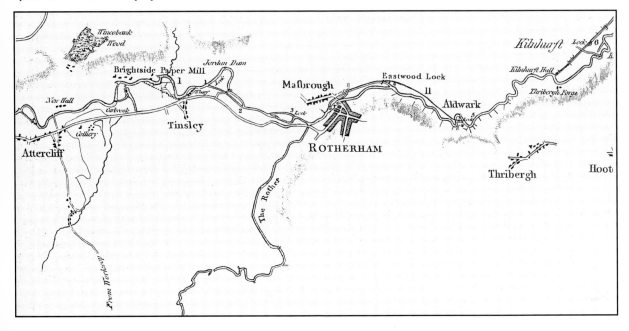

40 The arrival of the navigation at Rotherham persuaded Samuel Walker (1716-82) (seen here) with his brothers Jonathan and Aaron, to move their iron founding business from Grenoside, north of Sheffield, to Rotherham. Such was Samuel's business acumen and energy, that the Walkers' works soon became one of the leading iron and steel concerns in the country. [988]

41 The Walkers established their first factory, known as the Cupola Works, close to the canal at Masbrough. Some of their buildings still exist and are shown here as they were in 1971. [3782-3]

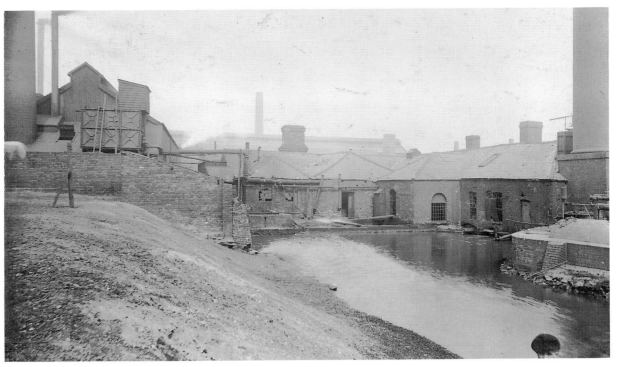

42 As their business prospered, the Walkers leased a large part of the Holmes estate from the Earl of Effingham. Their works included blast furnaces, steel works, foundries, tin plate works etc. Shown here in the late 19th century, the rectangular furnace chimney in the centre is a survival from the Walker era and was not demolished until the 1980s. [2760]

43 The layout of the works at the Holmes is shown in this map of 1822. 'A' marks the blast furnaces. At the eastern end of the Mill Dam, 'K' was a rolling mill, slitting mill and boring mill, 'I' was the old rolling mill, 'G' a boring mill and plate warehouse, 'H' the tin house, tinned plate warehouse and scouring room and 'M' the house known as the Holmes.

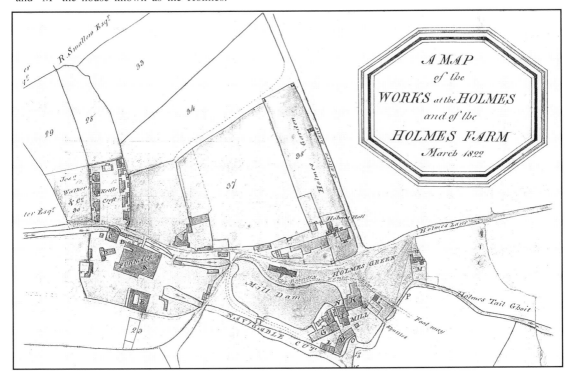

44 (*above*) The Walkers perfected the difficult art of casting and boring cannon and became important suppliers to the Royal Navy. Walker cannon can be seen on board HMS *Victory* and at Edinburgh Castle. This example was on board the brig HMS *Weazle* which sank in the Bristol Channel. It was raised in the 1960s and is now owned by retired local businessman, Dennis Grayson.

45 (*right*) The Walkers were also famous for their iron bridges. The largest was John Rennie's Southwark Bridge across the Thames, completed in 1819. In financial terms the bridge was a failure and the Walkers were never paid in full for their work. The Walker bridge across the Ouse at Newport Pagnell remains in daily use. [Guest, J., *Historic notices of Rotherham* (1879)]

46 (*right*) The second generation of the Walker family were as much landed gentry as industrialists. Joshua Walker I (1750-1815), son of Samuel Walker I, built Clifton House, and was the main partner in the concern after his father's death in 1782. [980]

47 An early 19th-century view of Rotherham, based on a painting by William Cowen. The artist has seated himself at the confluence of the Rother and Don. The chimneys to the right of the bridge mark the site of an 18th-century pottery, converted into an iron foundry in the 19th century. [John Guest, *Historic notices of Rotherham* (1879)]

48 Supported by public subscription, the Rotherham Dispensary was founded in 1806 to 'provide medical aid and service, particularly the treatment of accidents ... within one mile of the Parish Church'. It moved to this new building in College Street in 1828. Next door was the Grammar School and subscription library. The Assembly Rooms can be glimpsed at the rear of the Dispensary. [2144]

49 Ebenezer Elliott (1781-1849) was born at the New Foundry, Masbrough, and educated at the Hollis School. Although the family iron foundry failed, he became nationally famous as a radical poet, the 'Corn Law Rhymer'. After a more successful career as an iron merchant in Sheffield, he retired to Darfield where he is buried. [715]

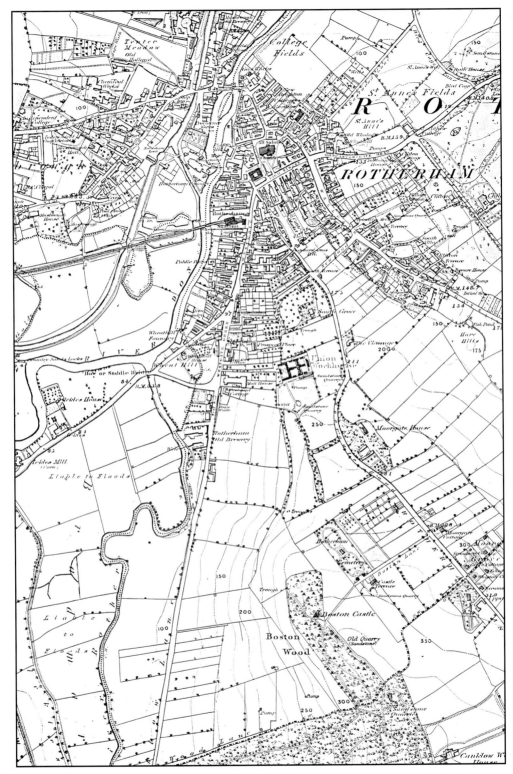

50 The Ordnance Survey 6ins. to 1 mile map of 1854 shows that the town centre had grown little since the late 18th century (see 38). A family settlement prevented the Earl of Effingham from granting leases of more than 21 years which stifled development. In 1850 he obtained a private act of Parliament allowing him to grant long leases and began to develop the College Fields area. [O.S. sheet 289, enlarged]

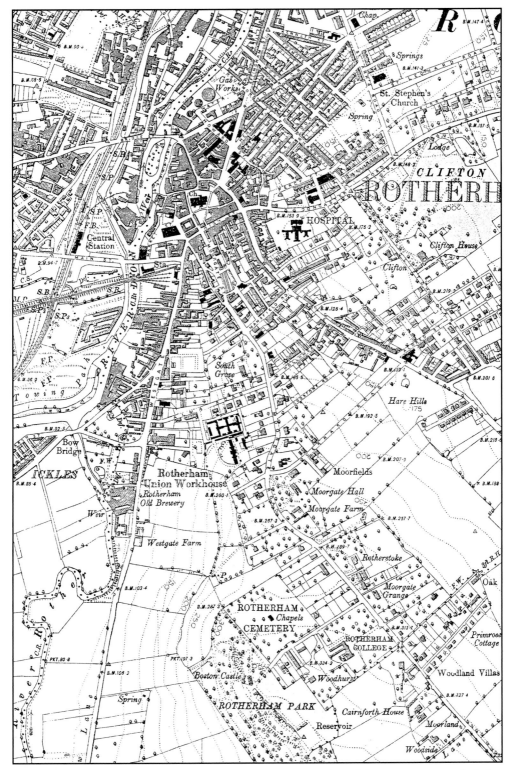

51 The 1890 Ordnance Survey map shows considerable expansion of the town centre, particularly towards the north east. Most of the streets in this area—Howard, Frederick, Effingham and Nottingham Streets—take their names from the Earl of Effingham's family. Development had also started in the Eastwood and Clifton areas. [O.S. sheet 289SE, enlarged]

52 This view would have met a traveller entering Rotherham from Sheffield in the 1860s. Taken from Westgate Green, it shows the western side of Westgate most of which has been demolished. Charles Payne is named as licensee on the sign of the *Travellers Inn*, dating the photograph from 1860-5. [161]

53 The earliest known view of the High Street, dating from 1860-4, shows how narrow the town's main street then was. The *Rotherham Advertiser* began life in the Caxton Printing Works (the low building in the centre) in 1858. A window cleaner is at work on Askwith's grocery shop (now Rumbelow's). [2315]

54 The medieval *Three Cranes* is prominent in William Judd Palmer's 1870s photograph of the High Street. The Georgian house next door, which had also been an inn (the *Swan*) became the home and offices of solicitor Thomas Badger in 1821. On the skyline are the spire of Rotherham Congregational Church (now the Civic Theatre) and one of the two windmills that stood on Doncaster Gate. [2317]

55 (*above*) This engraving of the intersection of the High Street, Wellgate, College Street and Doncaster Gate is based on a photograph taken *c*.1865. The low building beyond Scales and Salter is the *Elephant and Castle* while the *King's Head* occupies the corner of College Street and Doncaster Gate. [John Guest, *Historic notices of Rotherham* (1879)]

56 (*right*) By the mid-1890s the *Elephant and Castle*, Scales and Salter and the *King's Head* had all been rebuilt. The new branch of Williams and Glyns Bank, at the corner of Wellgate, dates from 1892. Judging from the clock and the shadows, the photographer had risen early to capture this view. [2313]

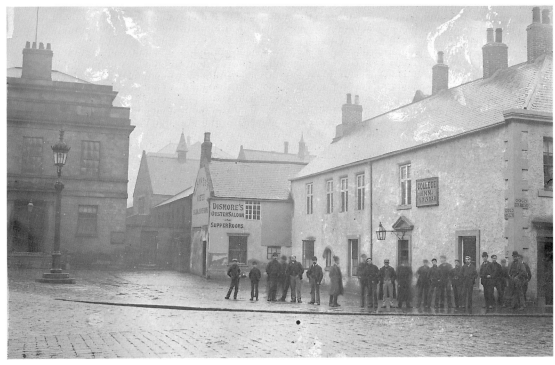

57 College Square was bounded by the *College Inn*, the Court House, Effingham Street and College Street. William Pindar was licensee of the *College* from 1891-7. The Court House (left) was erected in 1828 and demolished a century later. The roofs of the parish church schools are visible beyond Dishmore's Oyster Saloon. [2170]

58 The Dispensary could offer only out-patient services and anyone needing in-patient treatment had to be taken to Sheffield. By the 1860s there was a crying need for Rotherham to have its own hospital. Fund raising began in 1867 and the Rotherham Hospital on Doncaster Gate was opened in 1872. [2619]

59 Photographers did not often venture into the ill-lit courts of cramped, insanitary houses that lay behind the shops in the town centre. This is Garden Row, Wellgate (later Court 20) in the 1880s. In 1881 one of these small cottages was home to five adults and seven children. Garden Row was demolished *c*.1919. [190]

60 With the expansion of population in the 19th century, it became impossible for the parish church to minister to such a large parish. St Stephen's Church on St Ann's Road was erected in 1873-4 to serve the growing Eastwood area of the town. A spire with a peal of bells was added by Sir Charles Stoddart in 1910. [4314]

61 The second Wesleyan chapel on Talbot Lane remained in use until November 1901 when the chapel burned down after an organ tuner dropped his candle into the organ. Although the volunteer fire brigade was on site within 15 minutes, the building was gutted. The congregation began fund raising immediately and the third Talbot Lane Chapel was opened in 1903. [3028]

62 James Yates (1798-1881), a cousin an employee of the Walkers, took over their foundr interests in 1823 in partnership with Charle Sandford. They ran the Phoenix Foundry o Greasbrough Road, and the Rotherham Foundry o Domine Lane. The partners split in 1838 and i 1846 Yates formed Yates, Haywood and Co. i partnership with George Haywood and Georg Drabble. [993]

63 In 1855 Yates, Haywood and Co. opened new factory at Masbrough. Effingham Works wa claimed at the time to be the largest factory of it kind in the world. Its Thames Street frontage is sti impressive, despite having lost 100 feet to the inne ring road. [4099]

64 Expanding Victorian towns had an insatiable demand for kitchen ranges and fireplaces. This example of Yates, Haywood and Company's patent 'Quadrant' kitchener was installed in Ferham House in the 1870s. A range like this would have cost around £18. [4798]

65 By 1859 James Yates was able to build himself a mansion, Oakwood Hall, on the outskirts of the town. During the First World War the house was used as a V.A.D. hospital and after 1919 it became a T.B. sanatorium. Oakwood Hall now houses the headquarters of Rotherham Health Authority. [8955]

66 Richard Chrimes (1819-97) was the brother of Edward Chrimes jnr., a Rotherham plumber and glazier who patented the modern screw-down tap in 1845. After Edward's death in 1847, Richard came back from London to take over the family's Butter Market brass foundry, taking John Guest into partnership. [663]

67 John Guest (1799-1880) was a clerk at the Phoenix Foundry when he joined Richard Chrimes to found Guest and Chrimes. A heavy drinker in his younger days, Guest reformed after a serious road accident. Both he and Chrimes were ardent advocates of temperance. [13]

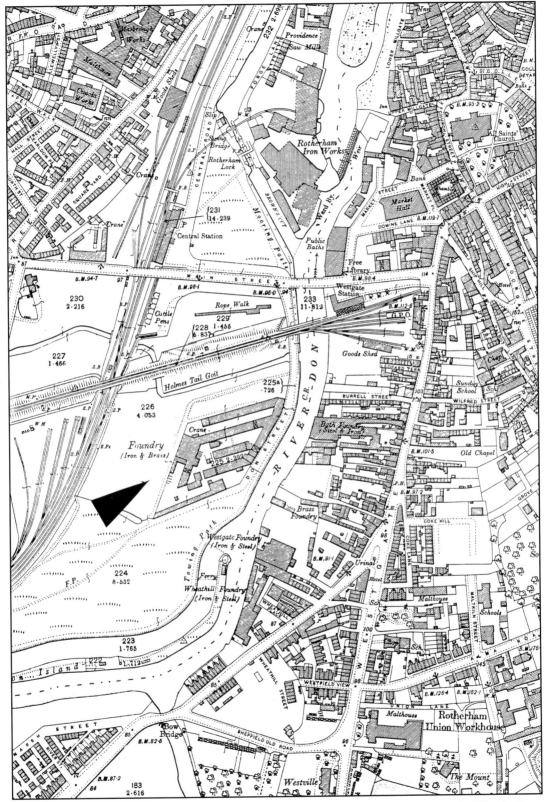

68 In 1857 Guest and Chrimes moved from the cramped Market Place foundry to a new building in Don Street, Masbrough. The Main Street bridge over the Don had not then been built and much of the machinery was moved by boat (see also 114). The factory is still in use. [O.S. 1:10560 (1890)]

69 The tower of John Guest's mansion is still a landmark on Moorgate. Guest first built himself The Cottage, at the top of Moorgate Grove, in the 1840s. In 1862, he bought Moorgate Cottage, extending it to create Moorgate Grange, seen here *c*.1870. [13]

70 The first forge on Forge Island was founded by the Walkers in the mid-1750s. In the 19th century the works, then known as Rotherham Forge and Rolling Mills, were famous for forging and turning large crankshafts. A number of part-finished crankshafts are visible in this view of the turning shop *c*.1910. [4880]

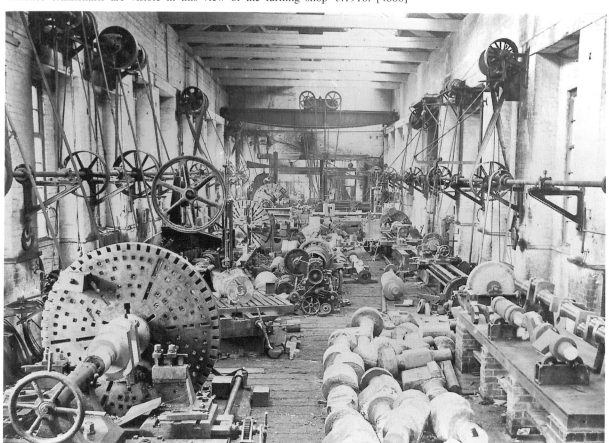

71 The tool makers Peter Stubs established a steel works in Masbrough to provide high grade steel to their factory in Warrington. In 1842 they purchased and demolished Holmes Hall to erect this imposing factory, Warrington Works. The chimneys mark the six cementation furnaces. [2736]

72 An interior view of the Templeborough Melting Shop and its fourteen 80-ton open-hearth furnaces. Erected by Steel, Peech and Tozer in 1917 to meet wartime demands for steel, the melting shop served until 1960-2 when six 100-ton electric-arc furnaces were installed. [112/B]

73 It was the practice at Steel, Peech and Tozer to take regular group photographs of the workforce. These were the workers in the Foundry in 1909. The boy seated at the front was Joe Foster whose father is second from the left in the middle row. [112/B]

74 Teeming molten steel from a 100-ton ladle into ingot moulds at Templeborough Melting Shops *c*.1950. The ingots would later be rolled into billets and bars or drawn into wire. [6145]

75 Among the early Rotherham companies producing railway wheels was Owen's Patent Wheel, Tire and Axle Co. at Phoenix Works, Greasbrough Road. This photograph from the 1870s shows how the spokes were formed from wrought iron bar inside a circular jig. A hub would then be welded into the centre and a tire shrunk onto the outside. [112/B]

76 The Fullerton Road firm of Owen and Dyson, founded 1875, established an extensive export trade with the Colonies, India and South America. These wheel and axle sets were awaiting export to India in 1880. [112/B]

77 With coal seams close below the surface, it was inevitable that Rotherham would become a mining centre. The introduction of steam engines for winding and pumping enabled ever deeper seams to be exploited. Holmes Colliery worked several pits in the Garrowtree area of Kimberworth. A new winding-engine house, drawn by Joseph Pearson, was erected in 1830.

78 Larger and deeper pits were sunk in the later 19th century. Rotherham Main Colliery was sunk alongside the Rother at Canklow in 1890 by the Sheffield steel makers, John Brown and Co. Closed in 1954, few traces of the pit now remain. [1302]

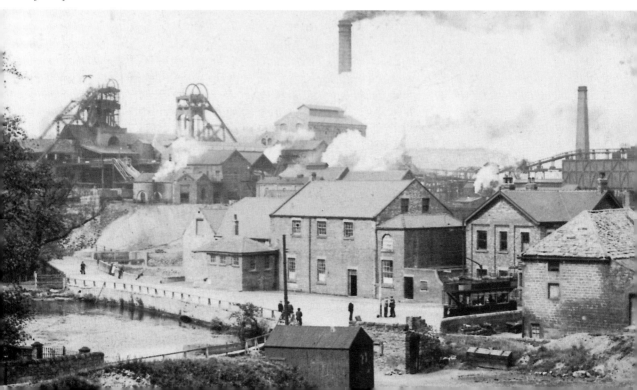

79 The presence of coal and clay led to the establishment of a number of potteries in the Rotherham area. Holmes Pottery, adjoining Holmes Station, was established by Thomas Jarvis *c*.1850. Domestic earthenware was produced until the early 1930s. [5245]

80 Some of the workers at the Holmes Pottery were housed in these grim-faced houses in Pottery Row. The pottery's clay mill can be glimpsed at the bottom of the street. The houses were demolished in 1919. [5614]

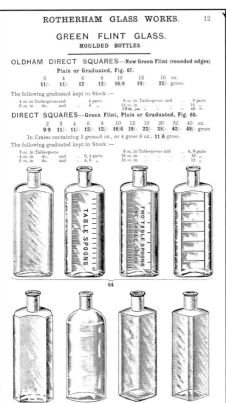

ROTHERHAM GLASS WORKS.   12

GREEN FLINT GLASS.
MOULDED BOTTLES.

OLDHAM DIRECT SQUARES—New Green Flint (rounded edges)
Plain or Graduated, Fig. 67.

3	4	6	8	10	12	16 oz.
11/-	11/-	12/-	12/-	16/6	19/-	22/- gross.

The following graduated kept in Stock :—

4 oz. in Table-spoons and   4 parts   8 oz. in Table-spoons and   8 parts
6 oz. in   do.   and   6   „   12 oz. in   12   „
                                                    10 oz. ..   16   „

DIRECT SQUARES—Green Flint, Plain or Graduated, Fig. 68.

2	3	4	6	8	10	12	16	20	32	40 oz.
9/9	11/-	11/-	12/-	12/-	16/6	19/-	22/-	28/-	42/-	49/- gross

In Crates containing 5 gross 6 oz., or 4 gross 8 oz., 11/6 gross.

The following graduated kept in Stock :—

3 oz. in Table-spoons   6, 8 parts
4 oz. in   do.   and   3, 4 parts   8 oz. in Table-spoons and   6, 8 parts
6 oz. in   do.   and   4, 6   „   10 oz. in   10   „
                                            12 oz. in   12   „

64

65   66   67   68

81 The present glassworks of Beatson Clark plc are a direct descendant of the works established by John Wright in 1751, which were leased to John Beatson in 1783. This view of the glassworks is pre-1870, before the railway was built between the factory and canal. The six glass cones gives an indication of the works potential output.

82 A page from the 1901 Beatson Clark catalogue, illustrating some of the great variety of bottles that they made. [307/B]

83 The large number of public houses in 19th-century Rotherham required a steady supply of beer. Mappin's Masbro' Old Brewery, established in Greasbrough Road in 1835, was purchased by John Newton Mappin in 1849. Mappin's beers helped to quench the thirst of local workers until 1958. The workforce were photographed in the works' yard at the turn of the century. [8949]

84 The Rotherham Markets Act of 1801 also established a Company of Proprietors of Rotherham Market. In 1804 the Proprietors replaced the old Shambles with this stone building with 28 shops on the outside and 20 butchers' stalls around an interior courtyard. The Shambles and Market Place, along with the market rights, were taken over by the Local Board in 1869. [2969]

85 The *Old Blue Bell* and the *Nag's Head*, together with the Corn Exchange (right) were among the properties demolished to make way for the town's first Market Hall, opened in April 1879. The Market Hall was gutted by fire in 1888 and a new Hall constructed in 1889. [2971]

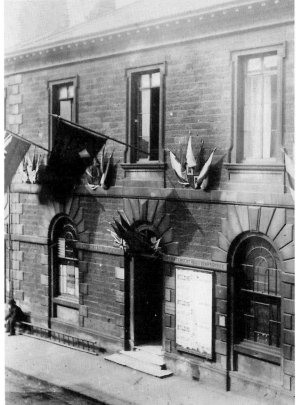

86 One of the first buildings to be erected in Howard Street was the offices of the new Local Board of Health, constructed in 1853. Taken over by the Borough Council in 1871, the offices are seen here decorated for the Prince of Wales's visit to open Clifton Park in 1891. [6]

87 John Matthew Habershon (1824-94) was typical of the solid Victorian businessman who saw public service as a duty. He served several years as chairman of the Local Board of Health and was elected as the town's first mayor in 1871, serving for two years. [816]

88 The town marked Queen Victoria's Golden Jubilee by erecting this combined Public Baths and Library at the corner of Main Street and Market Street. It was opened in June 1887 but the Library was not ready until the following year. The Library was gutted by fire in 1925 but, despite constant problems with leaks, the Baths remained in use until 1968. [4]

89 By 1895 the original Town Hall had been expanded and rebuilt, incorporating the Savings Bank next door and the Mechanics' Institute at the corner of Effingham Street. The new courts at the corner of Frederick Street were built on the site of the original Zion Chapel. [2772]

90 Since the Middle Ages the Monday cattle market had been held in the area known as the Crofts, above the High Street. At one time it was the largest beast market in southern Yorkshire and drew sellers from Lincolnshire and buyers from Lancashire. The newly-built Talbot Lane Chapel was photographed across the cattle pens *c.*1905. [4537]

91 The Rotherham Gas Light and Coke Company, established near the Bridge in 1833, was taken over by the Local Board in 1870. The retorts and condensers are shown in the course of demolition in 1933 after the Corporation found that they could supply the town's needs with gas from local steelworks. The bus station now occupies the site. [4963]

92 When the Local Board took over the Rotherham Water Company in 1852, they built a pumping station on College Fields to improve the supply. A second pumping station (shown here *c*.1905) was erected at the far end of Doncaster Road in 1887 to pump water from the Dalton Brook and Aldwarke spring. From 1903 it was the terminus of a tram service from town. [6295]

93 The town's volunteer fire brigade was reorganised as a permanent force as a result of the destruction of Talbot Lane Chapel in 1901 (see 69). The horse-drawn Merryweather steam fire pump was kept at the depot in Rawmarsh Road. The first motor fire engine was purchased in 1914. [4839]

94 Rotherham appointed its own police force in 1882 and new headquarters were erected on Frederick Street in 1895. The yard at Frederick Street was the venue for this photograph of the force *c*.1910. The Chief Constable, Edwin Weatherhogg, seated fifth from the left in the second row, joined the force as a constable in 1887 and rose through the ranks. [7059]

95 The Corporation were always ready for a good parade. In June 1911 they proceeded from the Town Hall to the Church to celebrate the coronation of George V. The band of the 5th York and Lancs are just disappearing out of shot, followed by a troop of the Royal Horse Artillery, with the Deputy Mayor bringing up the rear in the far distance. The Mayor himself was in London. [8009]

96 The construction of a new Court House in the Crofts in 1926-7 necessitated the removal of the Cattle Market to Corporation Street. The new market is nearing completion in this photograph of 1926. The Cattle Market finally closed in 1967 and Riverside Precinct now occupies the site. [2205]

97 A busy afternoon in the High Street, captured by the photographer *c.*1910. A tram from Templeborough has just reached the bottom of the hill while a carriage with liveried coachman pulls away from the roadside outside J.J. Humphrey's pawnbroker's shop. [4524]

98 This view of Westgate is taken from a similar viewpoint to 52 but is some 40 years later. The *Travellers Inn* is still prominent (it closed in 1909) and a tram makes its way towards the Canklow terminus. [152]

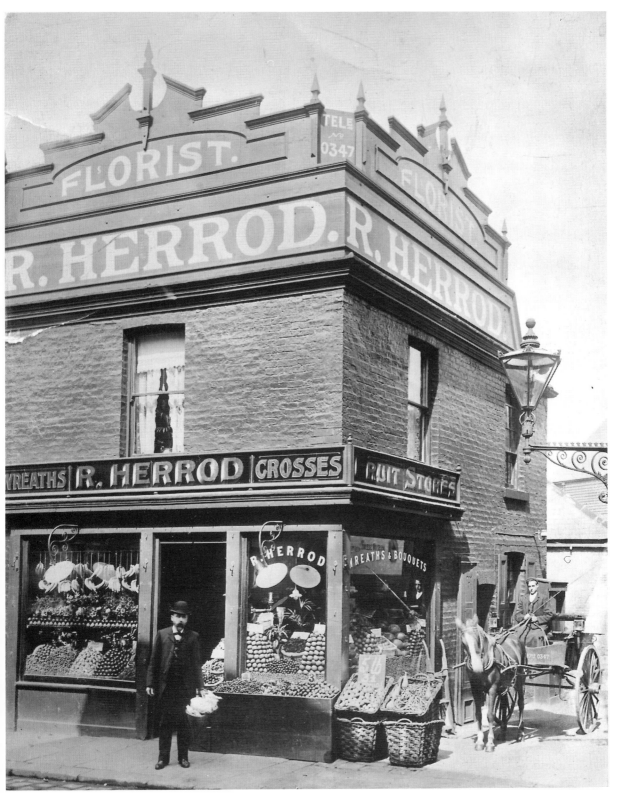

99 R. Herrod poses in front of the meticulous displays in his greengrocer's shop at 11 College Street while his delivery man poses in the yard. Note the telephone number prominently displayed. The first telephone service in the town was run by the National Telephone Co. Ltd. and reached 400 subscribers in 1887. [2108]

100 (*above*) On a sunny Edwardian afternoon Sheffield tram 74 sits outside the *Falstaff* in Effingham Street awaiting passengers for Sheffield. Note the elaborate gas lamp in College Square. Beyond the Court House is St George's Hall, founded in 1878 as a centre for church work and friendly society meetings. The cost was born by Rev. William Newton. [4514]

101 (*right*) The numbers of people walking down St Ann's Road, *c.*1912, suggest that they have just left an event in Clifton Park. At the far end of the road can be seen the large waste tip known popularly as 'Mother Kush' or 'Spion Kop'. This lay to the rear of the refuse destructor at Northfield. [8660]

102 (*above*) Moorgate Road was Victorian Rotherham's stockbroker belt. At the extreme left of this view *c*.1905 is the Plymouth Brethren's meeting room, built by Richard Chrimes (see 66) in 1875. It later became the Parish Hall. Beyond four private houses is the building occupied by Rotherham Grammar School between the years 1857-90. [5699]

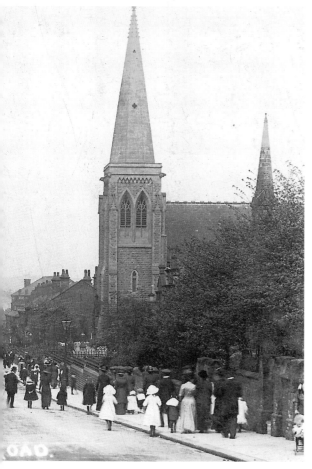

103 The Crescent, Doncaster Road, is a curved terrace of houses designed in 1902 by James E. Knight for the builder William Thornton. The architect himself lived at Brooklands, the detached house just beyond the terrace, but later moved into Crescent End nearest the camera. [3813]

104 Almost all the newly-built houses visible in Broom Road in 1905 were designed by the Rotherham architects Edward Hutchinson and Son (note the curved-top sash windows, their trade-mark). The developer was William Mullet, described as a 'warehouse man' in contemporary directories. [1251]

105 Rotherham's post office was housed in the former Westgate station building from 1880 until 1907 when this purpose-built headquarters was opened in Main Street. The elaborate telegraph poles on the roof mark the local exchange of the National Telephone Company next door. [2485]

106 The staff of the Main Street post office were photographed in the yard in 1914. Many of the younger men would soon be off to war. The names of the 19 who did not return are on the post office war memorial, unveiled in 1920 and now in the sorting office. [2479]

107 Crowds assembled in Effingham Square to see the unveiling of the Hastings Clock on 20 June 1912. The gift of local businessman James Hastings, the clock commemorated the coronation of George V. As it was driven by weights, a 14-ft. shaft had to be excavated underneath. [2435]

108 In the days before bottled milk, the milkman brought his churn to the door and measured the milk into the housewife's own jug. In the years before the First World War, Samuel Kent ran a dairy at Bradgate. His son, Edwin Kent, is standing at the pony's head. [847]

109 The outskirts of the town were well supplied with their own shops. Favell's grocery store on Masbrough Street displays a wide variety of Edwardian advertising. The reference to 'a woman can stop a Derby gee-gee' dates the photograph to 1913 when suffragette Emily Davidson threw herself under the King's horse. [3775]

110 In the early years of the century, the stretch of Masbrough Street between Orchard Street and Station Road boasted a grocery, pawnbroker, clothier, music warehouse, butcher, greengrocer, pork butcher, furniture broker, fried fish dealer, hair-dresser and two shopkeepers. [3778]

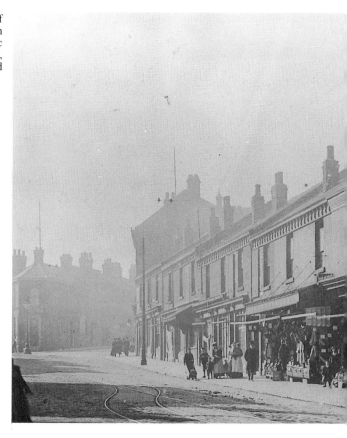

111 In the Edwardian summer of 1908, members of the 5th Battalion, York and Lancaster Regiment, embark at the Central Station for their annual camp. The 5th Battalion was the Territorial battalion of the local regiment which was to suffer heavy casualties in the war six years later. [6617]

112 (*below*) In April 1916 a civic reception was held in College Square for local heroes Pte. James Malia (winner of the Conspicuous Gallantry Medal at Gallipoli) and Signaller Clements (Distinguished Conduct Medal). Pte. Malia stands on the right hand of the Mayor, T.W. Grundy, with Signaller Clements on his right. The guard of honour was supplied by a heavy battery of the Royal Garrison Artillery. Raised locally in 1915, the battery was soon to leave for France. [3196]

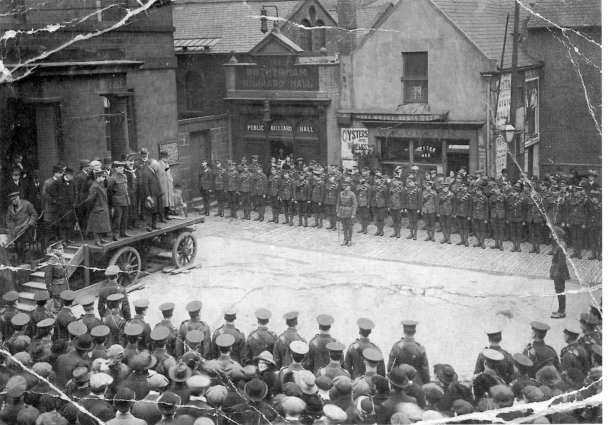

113 The toll house in Broom Road, controlling the Rotherham and Barnby Moor Turnpike, was at the edge of the town when it was built c.1826. By the time it was demolished in 1908, suburban development was spreading beyond it. The purpose of the tower at the rear of the toll house is unclear. [1246]

114 A typical Yorkshire keel is moored on the Don, near its confluence with the Rother c.1860. Guest and Chrimes's new factory dominates the background with Wheathill Foundry on the right bank. A new cut from the Don to Jordan, starting in the centre of the picture, was made in the mid-1860s. [7080]

115 Fifty people, many of them children, were drowned on 5 July 1841 when a barge being launched from Providence Dock, Masbrough, overturned, precipitating the crowd of spectators on board into the canal. The artist of the *Penny Sunday Times* and *People's Police Gazette* had obviously never seen a Yorkshire keel when he engraved his impression of the disaster.

116 In September 1931 heavy rain led to extensve flooding in Rotherham. The petroleum barge *Michael*, attempting to return to Goole, was swept over the weir and fetched up against the newly-opened Chantry Bridge. The Corporation used winches and steam rollers to haul the barge clear.

117 There were a number of early colliery tramways serving the pits around Rotherham. This house at Holmes controlled a rope-worked incline connecting coal pits in the Garrowtree area of Kimberworth with the canal at Jordan. [5253]

118 The first railway into the town, the Sheffield and Rotherham, opened in October 1838. The Rotherham terminus in Westgate is shown in this view of *c*.1870. Note the timber bridge over the Don and the Dutch barn-type train shed. This was unpopular with passengers and was soon replaced with a modest timber station building on Main Street. [6636]

119 The North Midland Railway from Derby to Leeds was opened through Rotherham in 1840 with a station at Masbrough. In the years before the First World War, a solitary passenger waits patiently while a train from the north approaches the opposite platform. [6595]

120 Rotherham's third station, on the Manchester, Sheffield and Lincolnshire (later Great Central) line to Doncaster, was opened in 1868. Three pairs of horses were needed to deal with this heavy load in the Central goods yard *c*.1910. The gentleman in the straw boater is William Wormald, the goods agent. [6616]

121 Modern public transport came to Rotherham on 31 January 1903 when the first trams ran on the lines to Fitzwilliam Road and Rawmarsh Road. This photograph was probably taken the previous day during an inspection run. David L. Winter, chairman of the Tramways Committee, is at the controls of Tram no. 1. [3995]

122 In October 1912 Rotherham instituted a trolleybus service from the Broom tram terminus to Maltby and became the first council to operate trolleybuses outside its own boundaries. The first three 28-seater Roe trolley buses, known locally as the 'Trackless', are seen here at Broom on the first day. [3766]

123 By the mid-1930s trolley buses had taken over a number of routes from trams and were running through to Conisbrough over the Mexborough and Swinton system. One passenger is anxious to disembark from Guy BTX six-wheeler no. 44, new in 1929, as it approaches the end of its run in Effingham Street. [6492]

124 Rotherham Corporation purchased its first two Daimler B-type motor buses in 1913 to run a service to Thorpe Hesley (fare 3d.). A third was acquired in October 1914 for a Canklow-Treeton service. The third bus was brand new when it was photographed outside Wickersley School on a private charter. [6478]

125 This building on the Crofts, now a public house, was constructed as the Feoffees' School in 1776. It provided education for 28 boys and 20 girls who were supplied with a distinctive Bluecoat uniform. Taken over by the School Board in 1893, it closed in 1896 when the new Alma Road schools were opened. [2252]

126 From its formation in 1875 the Rotherham School Board set about correcting the deficiency in education by building schools throughout the Borough. As the inscription on the gable tells us, the Board School in Alma Road was opened in 1896. The school closed in 1972-3. [4483]

127 Some of the pupils of Doncaster Road Infants School (now East Dene School) posed for the photographer in the 1930s. [4432]

128 Rotherham Grammar School moved to this building in Moorgate Road in 1857. The accommodation consisted of a single large schoolroom at the left with the master's house at the right. The school building, minus clock tower and turret, is now used as offices. [5784]

129 In 1890 the Feoffees were able to purchase the buildings of Rotherham Independent College (erected in 1876 at a cost of £26,000) for a mere £8,000 as a new home for the Grammar School. Since 1967 the buildings have housed Thomas Rotherham Sixth Form College. [4530]

130 The High School for Girls began as a private school in Alma Road. Taken over by the Borough Council in 1903, new buildings were erected in Middle Lane in 1910. In 1967 it became Clifton Comprehensive School. [3058]

131 The first higher elementary school in the town was opened at South Grove, Moorgate in 1911. It took pupils from the ages of 11 to 14, housing boys and girls on separate floors, and was well equipped. This is the metalwork room in the 1920s. The teacher, H. Radcliffe, stands in the background. [5854]

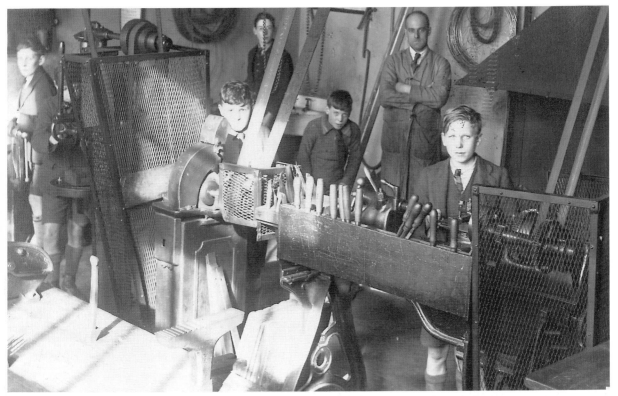

132 The names of 1,304 local men who gave their lives in the First World War are recorded on the war memorial in Clifton Park. Designed by local architect J.E. Knight, who had himself seen active service, the memorial was unveiled on 26 November 1922. Lt. Gen. Sir Ivor Maxse is seen here taking the salute with Dr. L.H. Burrows, Bishop of Sheffield, at the left. [1975]

133 A pony and trap makes its way down Church Street on a sunny morning in the early 1920s. Imperial Buildings (opened in 1907) is visible at the top of the street while Eaton and Son, one of several pawnbrokers in the town, is in the centre of the picture. [1346]

134 A policeman stands at the top of the High Street, ready to direct the sparse afternoon traffic in the early 1930s. The clock on John Mason's shop had formerly hung outside the Daily Express building in Fleet Street. [2335]

135 The new *College Inn* is just visible at the extreme right of this mid-1930s view of Effingham Street. The *College* and the other property on the right-hand side of the street was redeveloped between 1930 and 1933. In the background the Advertiser building of 1930 stands on the site of the Electric Pavilion (see 159). [2421]

136 Bridgegate in the early 1920s was a very narrow street. In the period 1914-28 the whole of the left-hand side was demolished and rebuilt to a new building line. The three brass balls on Turner's (yet another pawnbroker's) are visible in the centre. The empty *Turf Tavern* languishes at the left. [1098]

137   Viewed from the Church roof in 1928, Bridgegate is in the final stages of widening, with the *Turf Tavern* in the last throes of demolition. The property in the right foreground would soon be demolished to form All Saints Square. [8709]

138   By the 1920s the Town Hall was becoming cramped and more office accommodation was needed urgently. The art deco Municipal Offices were erected on the south side of Howard Street in 1924 to ease the overcrowding. They were to last only until 1980 before they were themselves demolished to make way for shops. [2861]

139 The Chapel on the Bridge was finally restored and rededicated as a place of worship in 1924. By the 1920s the medieval bridge was becoming noticeably weak and had to be supported with wooden centring. The new Chantry Bridge was built alongside in 1930. At the same time the old bridge was reduced to its medieval dimensions and access was restricted to pedestrians only. [1500]

140 In 1923 the Prince of Wales (later Edward VIII) came to Rotherham to open the new 30,000kw turbo-alternator in the Power Station which was thereafter known as the Prince of Wales Power Station. [1234]

141 The new Central Library in Howard Street was opened in 1931 to replace the Main Street Library which had been gutted by fire in 1925. It must have appeared lavish at the time but barely 45 years later it had to be replaced with a new Central Library in Walker Place. [6723]

142 As a strong mining area, Rotherham was badly affected by the coal strikes of 1921 and 1926. Many miners made ends meet by digging coal from colliery waste tips. Car House Colliery had closed in 1920 but there was still a considerable amount of coal to be won from its tip in 1926. Digging was obviously a family occupation. [1312]

143 The municipal elections of 1928 saw the Labour Group take control of the Council for the first time. The members of the group posed proudly outside the Town Hall around the Mayor, Alderman Stan Hall. Seated in the front row is Cllr. Mrs. Frances Lindley Green who was to become Rotherham's first female Mayor in 1943. [8088]

144 Rt. Hon. Arthur Greenwood (Minister of Health in the Labour Government 1929-31) came to Rotherham to open the new old people's housing at Herringthorpe on 28 November 1931. The Mayor, Alderman Caine, watches the ceremonial opening of the front door. [657]

145 These houses in Thomas Street, Masbrough, were also swept away in 1933 clearances. The girl at the right is Nancy Gaynor and the family in the first doorway are Mr. and Mrs. Burdin with their son, Harold. At the end of the street was a slaughter house and the local children used to delight in letting out the animals on a Saturday night. [4096]

146 In the 1930s the Corporation embarked on a major slum clearance campaign and photographed much of the property that was to be demolished. The narrow entry between Alfred Percy Telling's Westgate Meat Store and John Wilkins's grocery and general store was the only access to Court 8, Westgate a row of 11 single-back, two-roomed dwellings. The site of this property, demolished in 1934, is now occupied by the BT telephone exchange. [144]

147 Sam Moreton was a well known character in Rotherham between the wars. He had several fruiterer's shops where he sold the ingredients of a good rabbit stew for 1s. (although it did not do to enquire too closely into the source of the rabbits). He did not succeed in his attempt to get elected to the Council. [6013]

148 Sam Moreton had a finger in many pies, one of them being this wrestling and boxing stadium at the north end of Effingham Street. This is from an album of official police photographs, taken in 1937, so it would appear that they did not look kindly on Mr. Moreton's activities. In 1945 he was sentenced to three years' penal servitude for breach of the rationing regulations. [2568]

VOTE LABOUR . FOR . SAM MORETON

SAM MORETON

ROTHERHAM

The Candidate who understands the Working Man's Requirements.

Printed and Published by J. Richardson, Wade Lane, Leeds.

149 Simpson's shoe shop at 111-3 College Road, Masbrough, went to town with this display of 'K' shoes in honour of the Silver Jubilee of George V in 1935. [2033]

150 The families whose homes disappeared in the slum clearances of the 1930s were rehoused in the new council houses on the East Dene estate. This view of Broadway East clearly shows how the road got its name. Note the mix of house types, characteristic of the estate. [61/C]

151 In the mid-1930s, when the council houses spread south of Badsley Moor Lane, the new roads were named after poets. One of the new roads in the 'Poets' was Sheridan Drive. Dalton Parva church is visible on the skyline. The fields in the background were themselves covered with council housing in the 1960s. [61/C]

152 Meadowbank Road, from Kimberworth to Meadowhall, was constructed in the 1930s to provide work for the unemployed. In this view the ruins of Jordan Colliery stand above the partly completed road. [61/C]

153 One of the largest developers of private houses between the wars was the builder, Oswald Parkin, who built large numbers of semi-detached houses along East Bawtry Road in the 1930s. The road, formerly Castle Lane, was in the process of being rebuilt as a dual carriageway when this photograph was taken in 1937. [8683]

154 A number of new public houses were constructed to serve the new developments on the outskirts of the town. The *Stag Inn*, at the intersection of Herringthorpe Valley Road and Wickersley Road, was not new but was reclad in Thirties style. [8685]

155 In December 1940 the Princess Royal (daughter of George V) visited Rotherham to review the local A.T.S. and Women's Voluntary Service. Lady Lawson Tancred is here seen greeting the Princess in Westgate station yard. [3154]

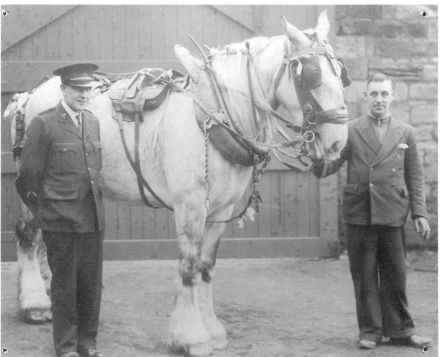

156 Luckily Rotherham suffered only two full scale air raids during the war. Twice in August 1940, the Luftwaffe tried to bomb the steelworks at Templeborough but hit houses in the Holmes Area. These houses in Josephine Road were damaged in the raid on 28 August. [3182]

157 One casualty of the air raids was this horse, injured when the stables of the Midland Ironworks were hit. The gentleman at the right is an R.S.P.C.A. inspector who came to examine the horse the day after the raid. [8053]

158 The Auxiliary Fire Service was one of many volunteer organisations that helped the war effort. The men of the Rotherham A.F.S. were photographed in the yard of the Fire Station in Erskine Road, which had been opened in 1939. [4844]

159 Effingham Street in 1952 looks little different to what it did in the 1930s (see 135). A close examination, however, will reveal that buses and trolley buses had ousted the trams and the 'keep left' sign in the foreground is sitting on top of the tram track. [2422]

160 Princess Margaret visited the town in April 1953. Members of the St John's Ambulance Brigade line the pavement in Church Street, while the Princess and the Mayor, Cllr. Maurice Young, talk to the Bishop of Sheffield outside the west door of the church. Her sister, Elizabeth II, was to visit Rotherham the following year. [6688]

161 When the flags came out for the Coronation in 1953, Bayliss and Taylor, newsagents, and William Wallace, grocer, were not left out. Even the Cadbury's advert on these shops at 383-5 Doncaster Road has a regal background. [3805]

162 Shaftesbury Square was part of a development of working-class housing erected in the 1850s. The houses were superior to many of the terraced houses in the town and they lasted until the 1960s. Mrs. Egley with her daughters, Wendy and Doreen, are standing in the doorway of no. 7 at the right. [4277]

163 The stone sets remained in the High Street until 1964. Most of the property visible here can be identified in the 1860s photograph seen earlier (picture 53). The photographer has perched on the scaffolding on the site of the new British Home Stores. [7788]

164 The 1960s were to see sweeping changes in the town with the construction of the inner ring road and the clearance of the houses around Norfolk Street. Among the property to go was this chemist's shop at the corner of St Ann's Road and Frederick Street. The building at the left was part of the former National School. [61/C]

165 The clearance of houses in St Ann's Road, Nottingham Street and Frederick Street revealed a clear view of the bus station in 1967. The new Central Library and other Council offices were erected on the cleared land in the 1970s. [6867]

166 Rotherham's traditional market place was in its last days when this photograph was taken in 1971. Over 700 years of history came to an end the same year when the Market moved to the new Centenary Market. A car park now occupies the site of the Market Hall. [2998]

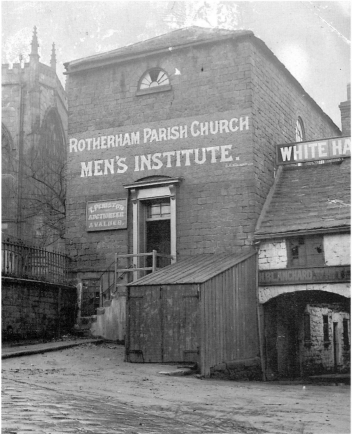

167 The Assembly Rooms, below the church, had a varied career as theatre, temporary Catholic church, auction rooms, Parish Church Men's Institute (as here *c*.1900) and billiard room. [2143]

168 In the early 19th century the Assembly Rooms provided a home for touring theatre companies. Unfortunately there were no local newspapers to tell us what local audiences made of *The Doubtful Son, c.*1800 or Miss Palmer's performance in *Presumptive Evidence* in 1835. [190/Z1/1,3]

169 Two of the town's places of entertainment stood close together at the junction of Henry Street and Howard Street. The Pavilion (previously the Electra Picture Palace) was originally Zion Chapel and was converted to a cinema in 1911. It closed in 1930. The much larger 'Hippodrome' opened as a variety theatre in 1908 and was converted into a cinema in 1932. It showed its last film in 1959. [2882]

170 The Regent on Howard Street began life as the Theatre Royal in 1894. Converted to a cinema in 1915, it became the Regent in 1930 and was turned back into a theatre in 1935. In its last years it survived on a diet of third-rate variety bills, strip-tease shows and local amateur performances. Closure and demolition came in 1957. [2872]

171 In 1876 the Corporation was able to lease Boston Castle and its grounds from the Earl of Effingham, creating the town's first public park. A feature of Boston Park was the surviving doorway from the College of Jesus which was re-erected against one of the rock faces. [794]

172 In 1891 the Corporation purchased Clifton House and its grounds. The grounds were converted into a park, opened by the Prince of Wales on 25 June 1891. The original bandstand served until 1919 when it was moved to Ferham Park. [1889].

173 Clifton House became Rotherham's museum, opened in July 1893. It was intended that the museum should be 'a centre of education and recreation combined' for the inhabitants of the town. [1993]

174 In the days before radio and television there was much self-made entertainment. The Rotherham Mandolin Band flourished *c*.1910. The leader, Percy Smith (extreme right rear), kept a shop/café at Ravenfield much patronised by cyclists. [8058]

175 Fishing has long been a popular pastime of the working man. This fishing party is about to set off from the *Eastwood Inn* on Doncaster Road *c.*1910. Their charabanc is a Sheffield-built Durham Churchill. [3814]

176 In 1936 the Corporation provided enhanced facilities for swimming by constructing new swimming baths in Sheffield Road. Beedens Ltd. of Thrybergh were the main contractors with steelwork from Dorman, Long and Co. of Middlesbrough and concrete floors from the Siegwart Fireproof Floor Company. [11064]

Selected Bibliography

'The Archaeological Survey at Canklow Woods, Rotherham', *Archaeology in South Yorkshire 1991-1992* (1992)

Armitage, Harold, *Rotherham's Forerunners* (1953)

Cockburn, J.H., *Rotherham Lawyers During 350 Years* (1932)

Copley, Harold, 'The Earthworks in Canklow Woods, Rotherham', *Transactions of the Hunter Archaeological Society*, vol. 6 (1950)

Crowder, Freda, and Dorothy Green, *Rotherham, its History, Church and Chapel on the Bridge* (1971)

Guest, John, *Historic Notices of Rotherham* (1879)

Guest, John, *Relics and Records of Men and Manufactures at ... Rotherham* (1866)

Gummer, George, *Reminiscences of Rotherham* (1927)

Hadfield, Charles, *The Canals of Yorkshire and North East England*, 2 vols. (1973)

Hopkinson, G.G., 'The Charcoal Iron Industry in the Sheffield Region', *Transactions of the Hunter Archaeological Society* (1963)

Hunter, Rev. Joseph, *South Yorkshire*, 2 vols. (1829/1831)

John, A.H., Minutes relating to Messrs. Samuel Walker and Co., Rotherham (1951)

May, Thomas, *The Roman Forts of Templeborough, near Rotherham* (1922)

Smith, Howard, *The History of Rotherham's Roads and Transport* (1992)

Woodward, R., *The Development of Education in Rotherham to 1944*, unpublished thesis